Fire Up!
For Learning

Active Learning Projects and Activities to Motivate and Challenge Students

By Randy Thompson
and Dorothy VanderJagt

Incentive Publications, Inc.
Nashville, Tennessee

Acknowledgement:

Thanks to Randy's father for teaching him to think
"out of the box," and to his son Jason for the "whys,"
"what ifs," and "why nots" that *keep* him out of the box.

Thanks to Dorothy's mom for keeping her fired up
about learning and life!

Cover Art By Geoffrey Brittingham
Illustration By Marta Drayton
Edited By Jean K. Signor and Jennifer J. Streams

Library of Congress Control Number: 2001094392
ISBN 0-86530-554-4

PRINTED IN THE UNITED STATES OF AMERICA
www.incentivepublications.com

It's my personal approach
That creates the climate.
It's my daily mood that
Makes the weather.

I possess a tremendous power
to make a child's life miserable or joyous.

I can be a tool of torture
or an instrument of inspiration.

I can humiliate or humor,
hurt or heal.

In all situations, it is my response
That decides whether a crisis
Will be escalated or de-escalated
And a child humanized or dehumanized.

Ginott

Table of Contents

Introduction

All students have had teachers that they loved and whose classes they enjoyed so much that they could hardly wait to get to class. Those meaningful and challenging classes with enthusiastic teachers motivate students by keeping them actively engaged in creative projects and dynamic classroom activities. The goal of the authors of this book is to help teachers FIRE UP their students for school success with interactive classroom activities.

Some teachers are totally committed to avoiding activities perceived as time-wasters; therefore, they often bypass opportunities for excitement and readiness for learning afforded by valid interactive activities. The activities in Fire Up! For Learning are definitely neither mundane nor time-wasters. Each activity is designed to be of high interest to and have meaning for the intermediate and middle grades student, and to develop skills essential for student success and well being. Adjectives like *challenging* and *meaningful* do not mean that the activities are devoid of fun. All of the activities are interactive, motivational, skill-based, student-centered, and engaging.

Each activity is carefully presented to help teachers and students get the most out of the activities with the least amount of preparation and effort. The direction pages clearly outline how to run and process each activity and to help teachers make the activities relevant and meaningful to students in a given setting. Each activity includes a list of materials needed, an explanation of how to set up the activity, and tips on how to run and process the activity. The aim of this book is to give teachers some great ideas for their classes with the least amount of hassle on their part.

It is our hope that the activities presented in this book will make a positive impact in every classroom where they are used. Remember, it is permissible to use the words *fun* and *challenging* in the same sentence. Let's FIRE UP FOR LEARNING!

Fire Up For Learning!
Motivating Classroom Activities At A Glance

1. **The Dream Classroom**
   In this activity students will create the perfect classroom. Students will list and share what the perfect classroom looks like, sounds like, and feels like. Students are challenged to help make their classroom a dream classroom.

2. **The Talking Alligator**
   This is a great activity to teach students how to participate in group discussions appropriately.

3. **Super Student**
   It's a bird, it's a plane, it's SUPER STUDENT! With the ability to leap over tall teachers in a single bound, this new super hero will save your school.

4. **Juggling It All**
   This activity shows how many things our students have to juggle. A group of students will juggle a number of objects and relate the activity to the real life juggling they experience. This is a great activity to introduce student planners.

5. **Line-Ups**
   Students line up using different characteristics, such as birthdays. Along the way, they learn about each other.

6. **Directions Quiz**
   How well do students follow directions? This lesson will provide some strategies to promote listening and comprehension.

7. **Shh! Quiet Line-Ups**
   Gather around, up or down. Quiet line-ups are similar to line-ups but without the noise. You may decide some days that this is just the activity you need.

8. **Round 'Em Up**
   Round 'Em Up and Put 'Em Together! *Round 'Em Up* will help teachers with some creative grouping techniques.

9. **Who's Who?**
   Who's Who in this Zoo? This activity is a great way for students to get to know each other and learn new information about their fellow classmates.

10. **Show Me Posters**
    Students will generate alternative assessments to traditional tests. The activity allows students to get actively involved in finding the best way to display what they know.

11. **The Ultimate Test Review**

    The visual learners, the auditory learners, and the kinesthetic learners will all be engaged in this interactive review process. This is a productive activity that actually makes the review process fun.

12. **Estimation Jar**

    Teachers can COUNT on this one! This is a fun weekly activity that allows students to practice their estimating skills.

13. **Test Your Thinker**

    This activity is for teachers who like to challenge their students. These stimulating thinkers add excitement to any day.

14. **Marker Boards**

    This is a powerful way to reinforce concepts or to review for tests. This activity encourages a productive class period with interesting discussion and results.

15. **Like-O**

    Do you like what I like? Do I like what you like? The *Like-O* game allows students an opportunity to know their classmates better.

16. **Brain Benders**

    Warm-up, extra credit, or in-class—use this activity however you desire. Brain benders are a fun way to challenge the mind.

17. **Perplexing People**

    Who are you? This activity opens the door for discussion and insight on many important people in the field of education.

18. **A Stick-Up KWL**

    Let's stick to it! This activity helps recall prior knowledge, to link that knowledge to what students would like to know, and to list what students have learned.

19. **Check Please**

    Let's try this together! *Check Please* is a method of working together and offering input.

20. **Corner Move**

    Corner Move is a way to get moving and learn information. You may use this as a get-to-know-you exercise or with a content focus.

21. **Get in Shape**

    Hold it right there! *Get in Shape* will help reinforce concepts taught in class.

22. **Equation Frustration**

    Equation Frustration requires some concentration and mental quickness. Students are asked to solve the equations.

23. **Think—Pair—Share It**

    What do you think? Let's share our ideas! Students are able to pair up and share their responses and discuss information.

24. **Run-Around**

Run-Around and learn today! This is a fantastic game to emphasize concepts, to review topics, and to reinforce curriculum.

25. **Write Like Paul Harvey**

Paul Harvey is a creative writer who generates curiosity and holds the attention of his readers. Students will find the stories fascinating while learning some interesting information.

26. **Outside the Box**

Yes, let's think outside that box! *Outside the Box* is a wonderful activity that promotes enrichment and challenges the students.

27. **The Great Houdini**

The students are connected together in pairs by a couple of ropes and have to try to find a way to get apart. Even Houdini would have had a tough time with this escape!

28. **Untangle the Tangle**

Anyone who has ever had to get the knots out of tangled cords or fishing line can relate to the challenge students will face in this activity as they have to remove knots from a piece of rope.

29. **Lend a Hand**

Students will create a human knot with a few added twists; then they will untie the knot.

30. **As Easy as Tying Your Shoe!**

Sure you can tie your shoe, but could you tell someone else how to do it? Students learn how difficult the art of communication really is. What we say and what we mean are not always the same.

31. **Squaresville**

The task appears simple. All the class has to do is form a square with a 50-foot piece of rope. That is, until they find out they all are to be blindfolded!

32. **The Plague**

Students get very involved and have a great time while showing how a plague or a rumor can move through a population quickly.

33. **Fire Brigade**

Pass the buckets! Or, in this case, the tablespoons! The students work as a fire brigade team to move water from one cup, using tablespoons, to fill another cup.

34. **Tubular Dude**

Students are challenged to work together to move bicycle tire tubes around the circle.

35. **Read-Alouds**

Entertaining stories with great messages to share with middle school students.

36. **The Team Puzzle**

In this activity, students become part of a puzzle and begin to see that they can fit in with their peers.

37. **All About Me**

Put the spotlight on me! *All About Me* focuses on students' thoughts and accomplishments.

38. **Directions Game**

Is anyone really listening to me? The *Directions Game* is a motivating activity that will help students pick up cues in their environment and recognize the importance of paying attention.

39. **Big Foot**

Students stack their feet in this problem-solving and team-building activity!

40. **Land Mine Clearing**

Students will become part of a specialized mine removal team, working together as they are challenged to cross a minefield in a simulated training mission. The students really get into this explosive activity.

41. **Have a Seat!**

Sit-ins will take on a whole new meaning after this activity. The challenge is to have the entire class sitting, without chairs, and not on the floor. You have to see this one to believe it.

42. **Fast Ball**

Students are challenged to move a ball in a particular order at ever-increasing speeds. This activity really requires creative problem solving, following directions, focusing on an outcome, and teamwork as the class goes for the world record.

43. **The Gator Swamp**

Working in groups, the students have to find a way to get their group across a gator swamp one person at a time. There are lots of gators in this swamp, and to make it even more challenging, the person crossing the swamp is blindfolded. Chomp! Chomp!

44. **Be a Brain**

Are you ready to enter the brain of an early adolescent? Students will build an early adolescent brain with their bodies, arranging themselves from the left to the right hemisphere according to their brain dominance.

45. **Java Move**

Let's enjoy some teamwork with a coffee can. Students will work together to solve a problem.

46. **Scavenger Hunt**

Which way do we go? The **Scavenger Hunt** allows students to discover techniques to encourage group collaboration.

47. **Love Those Lists**

Look at what we all know! This activity encourages brainstorming and working together to generate ideas and solve problems.

48. **The Leaning Tower of Pizza**

Building towers with edible materials like candy and marshmallows makes this activity a student favorite.

49. **A Pat on the Back**

We all deserve a pat on the back now and then. In this activity, the students give each other pats on the back that they can take with them.

50. **String Web**

You don't have to be a spider to get this one! Students create a web through their interaction with each other in this activity.

Getting Started

Team Building Activities to Fire Up!
Teachers and Students

The Dream Classroom

Any teacher or student who has ever dreamed of the perfect classroom will love this activity. By determining how such a classroom looks, sounds, and feels, the students will be on their way to making their own classroom the ideal one.

Materials needed

For each group, provide three pieces of chart paper or poster board and one marker.

Setting up the activity

Divide the students into groups of five or six. Ask them to share with their group members which classes and teachers they have really liked over the years and why. Tell them that today they are going to create a DREAM CLASSROOM.

Running the activity

First, the students need to imagine that they are visiting a variety of schools in search of the perfect classroom. As they are shown around each school, they will observe the classrooms through one-way mirrors. They will be able to watch, hear, and notice the feelings of the students and teachers in the classrooms, but they will remain unheard and invisible.

Next, tell the students to imagine everything they see as they look into the fantastic classrooms over a period of time. Then they are to write what they see on the first piece of chart paper. Remind them that they cannot hear a single word or sound in the rooms; they can only watch what goes on. If they were to watch over a period of time, what would they see that would tell them this is the best classroom of all time? Also ask the students to consider and record what things they would never see in a great classroom. When the groups are finished, move on to the next step.

In part two, the one-way mirror turns into a tape recorder. Help the students imagine that they will tape several ideal classrooms over a period of time. Then they will combine the tapes into one recording of the sounds of the perfect classroom. On the second piece of chart paper, have the students describe the sounds they hear that let them know which class is great. Remind them that they cannot see anything; they can only listen. As before, also ask the students to consider and record what sounds they would never want to hear in the classroom.

The third part might require more explanation. Move away from the one-way mirror and the tape recorder ideas, and help the students imagine that they can somehow observe the feelings of the students and teachers in the ideal classrooms. Thinking about their own experiences could help them with this part. They have all probably had classes and teachers that they really enjoyed. Ask them, "What does it feel like to go to a class you enjoy?" Their responses go on the third piece of chart paper. Answers here often include feeling wanted, safe, and challenged, the class is fun, the teacher cares about the students, and so on. As with parts one and two, also have the groups record what feelings do not belong in an ideal classroom. They might say things like fear and anxiety over the way the students behave or because of the way the teacher treats the students.

When the students have exhausted all three ways of describing the ideal classroom, direct the groups to put their three pieces of chart paper on the wall.

Processing the activity

Ask each group to present their three lists to the rest of the class. While listening to the different groups, create a master list that will have all the descriptors that were listed. The three master lists should be kept in the classroom or somewhere in the team area as a constant reminder of what a great classroom looks like, sounds like, and feels like.

Questions to ask and points to ponder

A helpful question for teachers to ask the students after this activity is, "What can you do to make our classroom reflect the characteristics on our lists?" There will always be descriptors that describe student behaviors. In fact, it may surprise teachers what a large percentage of each list are student behaviors. For example, in the dream classroom, it looks like students are focused on the teacher, come prepared, work well together, participate, are not disruptive, and so on. It sounds like the students are answering questions, are staying focused on the topic, are using appropriate voices, and are not being disrespectful to each other or the teacher. The classroom feels challenging because the students do their work; fun because there is camaraderie; safe because the students are not disruptive; and like a safe environment to take a risk because there are no negative comments by the students.

Throughout the school year, refer to the lists, and ask the students if they are adhering to the characteristics on their lists. If a teacher chooses to do this activity early in the school year, the students can use the lists to help create classroom rules. This is a great activity to help students become aware of their responsibilities in creating and maintaining the ideal classroom setting.

The next point to ponder is the teacher's part. The lists will note what the teacher does, or does not do, in the dream classroom. Occasionally reviewing the lists can help teachers as they prepare for their classes. The lists will often be pretty specific. For example, it looks like there are many activities, the teacher greets students at the door, the teacher smiles often, the teacher spends time helping students, the teacher does not sit at his or her desk but moves around; students have the opportunity to move around often, and so on.

For an ideal classroom's sounds, the teacher laughs, keeps students interested, does not lecture all the time, never puts students down, does not use sarcasm, encourages students, knows the subject, keeps students involved, and does not talk down to students. Students enjoy going to the perfect classroom because it feels like the teacher enjoys teaching. Students feel challenged but not intimidated by the teacher; they are not afraid to ask questions; the teacher makes the subject interesting and fun.

When planning lessons, teachers should keep this activity in mind. Ask three questions: What will this lesson look like? What will this lesson sound like? What will this lesson feel like? If teachers can get the students to understand their responsibilities from the lists and if teachers do their part, then all classes will look, sound, and feel more and more like DREAM CLASSROOMS.

The Talking Alligator

The Talking Alligator is an effective way to control a chaotic discussion. When anticipating a highly charged discussion or a discussion where everyone wants to talk at once, pull out the talking alligator. The talking alligator will help the members of any discussion group stay focused on the speaker and wait for their turns to speak.

Materials needed

Teachers may use small rubber alligators that can be found in the educational section of the dollar store. A variety of other animals may also be used; koosh-balls also work well. Use any object that suits the classroom, teacher, or students.

Setting up the activity

Use this activity any time there is the need for additional control during group or class discussions. Bring out one rubber alligator for each group, and designate who will begin speaking in each group by handing "Ali" to that student. Then, tell the students that only the person that holds Ali may speak. No one else may speak until he or she is holding the alligator.

Running the activity

Further guidelines may be suggested. Sometimes instruct the group that Ali must travel from left to right, or vise versa. Each student is expected to speak when Ali gets to him or her, and the students may speak only in turn. This way everyone in the circle knows who will speak next and that others cannot speak until they have Ali. They may not interrupt the speaker as they wait their turn to speak. This insures that everyone must listen until the person with Ali is finished. In some cases, it is desirable to put a time limit on how long anyone can speak, which will insure that Ali gets around more quickly and that no one can dominate the discussion.

Teachers can also let Ali move freely around the group. The same rule that no student may talk until he or she has Ali applies; the difference here is that there is no particular order to Ali's travels around the group. One of the additional rules here is that students must nonverbally ask for Ali when the speaker is finished to avoid interrupting the speaker. Everyone in the group must have held Ali once before anyone in the group gets Ali for a second time. This rule insures that everyone in the group speaks; two or three students cannot dominate the discussion.

Processing the activity

Some students will feel frustration with not being able to interrupt when they choose, while others will feel that it is the first time they have been fully included in a discussion.

Questions to ask and points to ponder

Teachers who use the talking alligator insure that everyone in the group has an opportunity to speak. Students express that it is nice to have a chance to speak. The opportunity to speak is important, and having a group's undivided attention is very empowering for students.

Each student has a responsibility to contribute to the group. There are students that have perfected hiding in groups or in class. Using the talking alligator forces each person to take a turn and add to the discussion. Students who know that they must talk are also likely to listen more carefully and keeps students actively engaged in the discussion.

This is an activity/strategy that can work well with adult groups. Native American groups used beautifully decorated "talking sticks." Only the person with the talking stick may talk. Whether using a stick, koosh-ball, rubber alligator, or some other object, **The Talking Alligator** is a great way to empower everyone to get involved.

Super Student

Try starting this activity by singing the old Army commercial jingle "Be all that you can be!" One teacher brought a standup cutout of Superman, but the S stood for Super Student! Superman can leap over tall buildings in a single bound and stop locomotives with a single hand; the purpose of this activity is to define all the things that Super Student can do.

Materials needed

First, obtain a roll of butcher paper or art paper. The butcher paper does not tear as easily as the art paper and therefore stands up better to student use. Markers and scissors are also needed for each group.

Setting up the activity

Create some open spaces to roll the paper out on the floor. A great way to create space for this activity is to move some of the chairs over to widen a couple of rows in the classroom. Tell the students that they are going to create the Super Man and Wonder Woman of students. Add or delete super heroes, as you like. Put the students into groups and place one roll of paper at the front of each row.

Running the activity

Ask one of the students in each group to volunteer to be the model for Super Student. That student will lie down on the paper, and someone should trace the model's outline on the paper. Some students do not want to be traced on the paper, but it is not difficult to get at least one volunteer to represent the group.

After each group has traced one or more of their members, the groups cut out their outlines. Then they are going to write on the cutouts. The group should complete the statement, "We could learn anything if we would or could just …", or "To be the best student, I would need to …".

Write the starter for the sentence on the board, and ask the students to complete the sentence on their cutouts. The goal is to get the students to think about all of the qualities that would make them the best student ever.

Give them some examples, and then let them record their ideas and suggestions on the cutouts. Tell students to include what they should and should not do in and out of the classroom. For example, students finish the sentence, "I could learn anything if I would or could just . . ." by writing the following: pay attention in class, follow directions, work well in groups, get enough sleep, have a place to do my homework, refrain from talking in class, eat breakfast, stay out of trouble, request homework help when needed, and respect others.

Processing the activity

As the students fill in their *Super Students*, have students decorate their cut-outs, and then post them around the room. Ask the groups to present their *Super Students* and share their characteristics they recorded with their fellow classmates. These figures are great to reference anytime a student needs some additional help and mentoring.

Questions to ask and points to ponder

How can a student embody super student characteristics? Have the students record their lists in their student planners as a reminder of their responsibilities. Organizational skills are required for many things on the various lists. Students begin to take a little more responsibility for their organization when they point out the need to be more organized. This activity also ties in nicely with the *Juggling It All* activity (page 21) to discuss how many things students have to juggle in daily life.

Another point that always emerges in the discussion is the role that the student plays in the responsibility of learning. Students are often quick to say that problems they may be having are the teacher's fault. If a student is struggling, ask the student to look over the lists generated during this activity to see if he is doing his best. Students are often able to identify the problem themselves and are able to work on a solution together with the teacher.

Teachers can help students set goals for becoming better students. Start by picking one or two items from this activity to work on. Celebrate the progress the students make toward performing at a higher level.

Kaizen is the Japanese term for continuous improvement, the relentless quest for a better way and higher quality, and the daily pursuit of perfection. Super Students, like Super Teachers, are always looking for ways to improve and practice kaizen. This activity gives the students a list of possible areas for improvement.

Juggling It All

Students have to juggle many activities and academic subjects to be successful in middle school. Try this activity early in the school year to establish the need and uses for student planners. This activity also begins to teach students how to focus and work in cooperative groups regardless of distractions. This is one activity students will request to do again and again during the school year; different skills may be highlighted each time it is used.

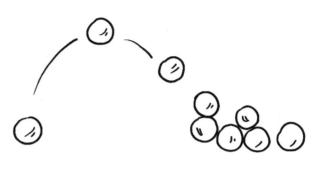

Materials needed

Ten to twenty objects appropriate for easy throwing and catching. All objects should be soft and easy to throw and catch. Soft plastic balls and/or koosh balls work especially well. The PE department may be able to provide objects (it is also fun to use rubber chickens and other unusual objects from time to time).

Setting up the activity

Begin this activity by putting the entire class into a circle. This activity works well for groups up to about forty students, but the activity becomes difficult with groups larger than that.

Provide an open area for this activity. The cafeteria works well, or if the weather is nice, this is a great outside activity.

Running the activity

Begin by picking a student to begin and run the activity. First, take one of the balls out of the bag and leave the bag behind the student. Then demonstrate how soft and harmless the balls are. Explain to the group that the starter is going to take the ball, call out the name of someone in the group, and toss it to that person. After the starter has selected someone, called his name, and tossed him the ball, go to that student and ask them to pick someone else in the circle, call out their name, and toss her the ball.

As the first three or four students do this, talk about appropriate throws, and remind them that the ball has to go to a different person every time until everyone in the circle has touched the ball one time. Each time students must call out the student's name before they toss the ball. After everyone in the circle has touched the ball one time, the last person will call out the starter's name and toss the ball back to that student.

After about the fourth toss, exit the circle and let the students continue the game. At this point, tell them that each person who has caught the ball should put her hands behind her, and anyone that has not should keep his hands in front of him.

The pattern will be random. After everyone has caught the ball once and the ball has made it back to the starter, have the students repeat sending the ball around the circle. This time they must call the name and throw the ball to the same person. It does not matter whom they choose the first time around, but now they must always throw to that same person. Practice at least once to make sure that students remember what to do.

Give the starter a ball to start the activity. After the ball has cleared the second person, give the starter another ball to start around the circle. After that ball has cleared the second person, give the starter another ball to start. Soon there will be many names being called at once and multiple balls being tossed across the circle. Keep adding balls until the balls are coming back to the starter faster than the teacher can add them. Let the activity continue for about five minutes before beginning to take the balls out of the circle. This activity gets very loud, and balls are flying everywhere!

When the teacher is ready to end the activity, stand behind the starter and ask him to put the balls back into the bag instead of continuing to send them around the circle. It can take several minutes to get all of the balls out of the circle.

Processing the activity

There are so many ways to process this activity that teachers and students will want to do it more than once during the year. In fact, students will often request to do it again and again. A great variation of this activity is to have the students send a ball around in reverse order. It is great fun to get a couple of balls going in each direction and to watch as the balls have to pass each other!

Questions to ask and points to ponder

This activity involves a randomly assigned pattern for throwing the balls. No one is told who to throw it to, many names are being called, and balls are going at the same time. How many times did mid-air collisions occur? One of the amazing characteristics of this activity is that with all of the juggling, there are very few, if any, mid-air collisions. As the discussion continues, ask the students how so many balls were juggled without hitting each other more often.

This question can lead into a discussion of teamwork, cooperation, the importance of following directions, and the ability to focus. Tell the students that they were actually on three-person teams: themselves, the person throwing to them, and the person to whom they were throwing. Each student had to focus on his or her team, while keeping an eye and ear on the other teams. This is a great activity to teach students how to work together in lab situations. They have to learn to focus on the task of their group while being aware of the other groups.

Pondering point two develops from the question, "What happened to the dropped balls?" When the students talk about picking up the balls for each other, ask, "How do people 'drop the ball' in real life?' Talk about how teachers, as well as students, drop the ball from time to time. Then ask how they can help others by picking up the ball for them. The impact of this activity can be significant; one class started homework pals after processing this activity.

Pondering point three arises from the question, Do students ever have to juggle more than one thing at a time? Ask students to list all of the things that they juggle. It is always amazing to see how many things students have to remember. They will list activities from school, such as homework (make them list all of the classes they might have homework in), sports, friends, and so on. They will also list activities from home, such as chores, babysitting, trips, church activities, sports practice, and the list goes on.

Then, ask how they keep up with all of these things. Some students will share that they do not always maintain everything very well. Talk about consequences of not doing some of the things on their list, such as homework or requests from their parents. This is when teachers should pass out planners to their students. Tell the students that a planner is something that might help them keep up with all of the things on their list. Ask the students to go through their list and check off all of the things that might go well in their planners. Of course, almost everything on the list, from homework assignments to friends' birthdays to church activities, can go into the planners. There is more student ownership when students record things from their own lists into their planners than when teachers or parents do it for them.

Line-Ups

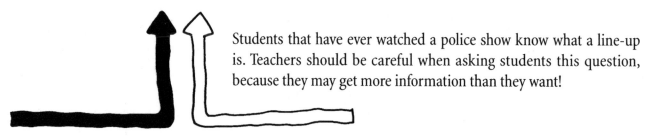

Students that have ever watched a police show know what a line-up is. Teachers should be careful when asking students this question, because they may get more information than they want!

Materials needed

A hallway or any area where all students can line up is the only requirement for this activity.

Setting up the activity

In the hallway, ask students to line up facing the teacher. Do not have them line up in any particular order.

Running the activity

Tell the students that they are going to change the order of their line-up as quickly as they can to get into the order the teacher requests. Each time the students line up, ask them to call out their information in order. Ask them to line up by their birth month, and then call out the months in order starting with January. Teachers can have students line up according to a variety of subjects that might be fun to share. Some of the characteristics teachers use to line up students include the following: their favorite food, the number of miles they live from school, their first names, their last names, their middle names, their favorite song or singer, their favorite NFL/NBA/NHL/MLB teams, or, for a real hoot, blindfolded by height, and so on.

Processing the activity

This is an activity that students process as they are doing the activity. Students and teacher can ask questions or share information after each line-up.

Questions to ask and points to ponder

The students always line-up by their last names the fastest. This activity is a great way to encourage students to share information in a non-threatening and creative way. This activity encourages students to call out answers and to listen to each other. It also is important for the teacher to share the information each time the students line up so the students can learn a little more about an important adult!

Directions Quiz

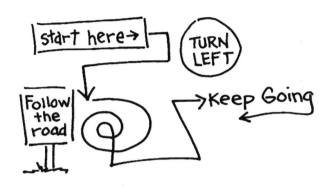

How many times have you heard, "I could teach if only they would listen?" Many teachers feel they repeat directions too many times throughout the day. Does this situation sound familiar?: "Okay, class, after the test, please put your tests in the test folder located on the back table." The directions were clearly given, right? The test folder has been in the same spot since August. Students have placed tests in the folder at least six times this year. So, why do these questions occur during the test? "Where do I put my test? What do I do with my test? Where is the test folder?" Then, lo and behold, at the end of class there are two tests on the teacher's desk. What is wrong here? Help!

Many times students *do* hear what teachers say. Sometimes it becomes a habit for them to continually ask questions. In a science classroom the teacher said, "Put your papers on the back table." It was surprising to notice how many students walked up to him and asked, "Where do we put these?" or, "What do I do with my paper?" or, "Is this homework?" He responded by asking, "What did I say?" and the inquiring students responded, "On the back table." The teacher was a little frustrated.

Other times students do miss directions; adults have this problem as well. Sometimes the directions are very clear and sometimes they may be a little confusing. It is a good idea to give directions orally to the students and have specifics written out on the board. Some teachers choose to write out the directions and give each student a sheet. This works especially well if the directions are multi-step or complicated. Some children are not auditory learners and need the directions written for clarification. Keep this in mind, particularly when assigning projects.

A good concept to teach children at any age is following directions. Students must listen in order to understand directions and improve comprehension. This is an important area to focus on especially in the beginning of the year. If students are aware of cues in their environment, they will be able to adapt to different situations easily. This lesson will provide some strategies to promote listening and

Materials needed

A directions quiz for each student (see page 27).

Setting up the activity

This activity works well with students, especially if the teacher does not allow students who follow all of the directions to give away the secret of the activity.

Running the activity

Pass out a quiz to students and tell them they may begin when they are ready. Wait as students begin the quiz. Some students will proceed with the tasks and a small number will actually figure out what they should be doing.

Processing the activity

This quiz demonstrates that directions need to be read. It is clear who reads the directions and who rushes through the quiz.

Questions to ask and points to ponder

This is a great opportunity to point out how we often hurry through a task without carefully reading the directions.

Many times during an assignment, quiz, project, or test, students do not read everything carefully, and they miss details.

This activity demonstrates how important it is to pay attention to detail. Often by reading the directions time is saved. Students share experiences at this point.

Quiz

1. Read every question before completing any activity on this quiz.

2. Put your name in the upper right-hand corner.

3. Circle the word upper in sentence two.

4. Draw three small triangles in the upper left-hand corner of this paper.

5. Put a T in each triangle.

6. Put a square around each triangle.

7. Sign you name under the title of this quiz.

8. After the word *quiz* write "show."

9. Put a circle around sentence six.

10. Draw a star in the lower left-hand corner of this page.

11. Draw a box around the star you just made.

12. On the back of this paper multiply 12 x 9.

13. Draw a circle around the word "quiz" in sentence eight.

14. If you think you have followed directions carefully to this point in the quiz, stand up and stretch.

15. On the reverse side of this paper add 9780 and 8756.

16. Put a rectangle around your answer, and then put a circle around the rectangle.

17. Make a crease in your paper by folding it in half vertically.

18. When you reach this point, yell out clearly, "I am almost finished!"

19. Cross out all even numbers on the side of the page.

20. Now that you have finished reading each question carefully, complete only sentences one and two.

Please do not give this quiz away by talking or laughing. If you have read this far, just pretend that you are still working. Let's see how many people really follow directions.

Shh! Quiet Line-Ups!

Quiet line-ups are similar to line-ups, but without the noise. Some days, this is just the activity teachers need!

Materials needed

No materials are needed for line-ups; however, be sure there is an area where students can line up.

Setting up the activity

Inform students that they will be forming a straight line in a specific order given to them by the teacher. There is one important guideline for the students to know: They may not talk as they line up.

Running the activity

Tell the students the order in which they are to line up. One line-up that works well is birthdays. Have students line up in order, starting with January, by their birthdays. Do not worry about the year they were born, just the month and day. There are many other topics to use such as number of pets students have, number of siblings in their family, number of letters in their last name, alphabetical order by last name and so on.

Processing the activity

Students will say their information aloud when they have formed the line. Begin with the first person and go through the line. Process the information as the activity goes along.

Questions to ask and points to ponder

This activity is an interesting way to share information without a lot of commotion in the classroom. Students are extremely creative; they will use their hands, the calendars, and visuals in the classroom to communicate. It is exciting for the students to learn about their classmates and their teacher. Teachers are encouraged to share with their students when processing the activity.

Round 'Em Up!

There are a variety of ways to group students. Some days teachers decide to group students with a common interest or ability. Other days they may opt for a heterogeneous grouping. Other times, students are placed randomly into groups. **Round 'Em Up** will help teachers with some creative grouping techniques.

Materials needed

A deck of cards.

Setting up the activity

Teachers need to decide how they are going to group the students.

Running the activity

Teachers may use **Quiet Line-Ups**. Have the students form a straight line. Once they have voiced their spot, have students fold the line in half. Pair students up this way, or ask them to fold the line over again for larger groups.

Another grouping method is to have students pick a card from the deck (you may eliminate face cards if you wish). Students need to remember their card since this card will be their card throughout the year. When assembling groups, randomly select cards from the pile into the number of groups required. If teachers would like to have groups predetermined without students knowing, simply "stack the deck." Just deal out cards from the deck into the desired groups.

Give students a choice of four animals—examples could include a horse, a cow, a dog, and a cat. Students select one of the animals and group themselves according to the animal they selected. Have students make the sound of the animal they select and ask them to group themselves accordingly.

Processing the activity

Teachers may choose to discuss probability; however, the activity's purpose is just to group the students. The processing will come when a task is given. For discussion, before the actual lesson, ask the animal groups to come up with a few reasons for selecting that animal.

Questions to ask and points to ponder

Determine how the students need to be grouped. If the method is totally random, there will be less preparation; however, if teachers desire that specific students be together, pre-plan the groups before the students arrive. The method by which they are grouped is often exciting for the students.

Who's Who?

Who's Who is a great way for students to get to know each other and learn new information about their fellow classmates. This is an excellent activity to use in the beginning of every year.

Materials needed

A *Who's Who* sheet for each student.

Setting up the activity

Prepare a *Who's Who* sheet for each student and make sure that every student has a writing utensil (see page 31). Students will be moving around in the classroom, so try to make the area free of obstructions.

Running the activity

Tell students that they need to find as many different students in the class who meet the criteria on the sheet as possible. The activity usually takes about ten minutes.

Processing the activity

Go though each question with the students. Ask students who they put in the blank and then ask for a show of hands of who could have fit into that blank. For example, a student may have marked Sally down for having blue eyes, yet there may be more students in the class who have blue eyes.

Questions to ask and points to ponder

Students enjoy sharing the information they have gathered. They also enjoy sharing information about themselves. Teachers need to keep control over the discussion, because students are eager to begin telling stories about their pet, travel, and so on.

This is an activity that involves all the students. A teacher may decide to be a part of **Who's Who**. Enjoy, laugh, and have fun with it!

Who's Who?

You will be gathering information from your classmates. Write the person's name in the blank when you discover someone who fits the category. You may use each person's name only once.

Find someone...

1. ...who likes playing basketball. _____

2. ...who has traveled to another state. _____

3. ...who has two sisters. _____

4. ...who has a dog. _____

5. ...who likes broccoli. _____

6. ...who was born in another state. _____

7. ...who enjoys swimming. _____

8. ...who has a cat. _____

9. ...who has jeans on today. _____

10. ...who is wearing red. _____

11. ...who knows how to make a batch of cookies. _____

12. ...who walks to school. _____

13. ...who likes pizza. _____

14. ...who has blue eyes. _____

15. ...who has brown hair. _____

16. ...who can stand on one foot for ten seconds. _____

17. ...who has seen a movie in the last week. _____

18. ...who plays an instrument. _____

19. ...who likes sports. _____

20. ...who knows a foreign language. _____

Fun
——— Curriculum Activities ———

Show Me Posters

Many teachers comment that students often express great frustration and anxiety with taking tests. Students profess that they have the knowledge even though they do not demonstrate it on the test. This activity will actively involve students in the assessment process and let them suggest ways they might be able to show teachers what they know.

Materials needed

Provide a piece of chart paper or poster board and a marker for each group.
Groups of 5 or 6 students work best.

Setting up the activity

Students are often frustrated by traditional tests. Start with a class discussion by asking students to share what makes test taking so difficult. After a discussion, put the students into groups of 5 or 6 and give each group a piece of the chart paper and a marker. Ask students to record on the paper alternatives to traditional tests. If they could choose any method to demonstrate their knowledge to teachers, what would they like to do?

Running the activity

Let them know it is completely up to them as to the means through which they demonstrate the knowledge. The idea is to fill up their piece of chart paper with as many ways as they can think of to show what they know. Share examples to get them started, such as working in groups, making an audio tape, making a video, making a collage, creating a skit, and so on.

One group of students demonstrated how they could show how the order of operations and the placement of parentheses work to change values in math class by creating "human equations." They gave each member of the group a piece of construction paper. A number or one parenthesis was written on each piece of construction paper in large print with a marker. The group was then told to create different values by moving around to correctly position the numbers and parentheses to give the correct value. Needless to say, many students preferred this *Show Me* activity to a traditional test.

Processing the activity

When the groups finish, make one composite list of all their suggestions on one **Show Me Poster**. The groups share how each one of the suggestions they came up with would work and why they might be better able to demonstrate what they know in this way rather than on a traditional test. As each group presents, encourage the rest of the class to discuss possible adaptations they might make and why the *Show Me* activity would be a good alternative to a traditional test.

Questions to ask and points to ponder

The point to ponder here is that students have a variety of learning styles, and different students might be more comfortable demonstrating their knowledge in ways other than through traditional tests. It is a great idea to occasionally let the students use the **Show Me Poster** for a test. Begin by letting the students know that the next test will be a *Show Me* activity. Prepare a traditional test for anyone that would like to take it.

Students will begin to think about how they want to SHOW the information as soon as they are told that the next test will be a *Show Me* activity. They will begin to accumulate pictures for a collage, or begin working with other students to put together a skit. Giving students some choice and even calling the test an activity instead of a test will take away some of the anxiety of the assessment process. The students will be more motivated and they will often work harder if they think they have some control over how they are being assessed.

When using the **Show Me Poster**, it is important to have a set of standards for what the students need to demonstrate regardless of how they decide to do it. Do not award one student a higher grade because he or she had a bigger poster than another student. Teachers need to be able to point out what components each student has or does not have to reflect their grade. Also, teachers may limit the *Show Me* options from the poster. Select 3 or 4 options for them to choose from this time, and give them other options the next time.

The **Show Me Poster** is an option to use only occasionally due to the amount of time involved. It will take students longer to complete and a teacher longer to evaluate. Teachers may receive as many different projects as there are students, and this can take considerably longer to evaluate since there is not one answer key. The extra time it takes is more than worth the improved student performance. Try to use a *Show Me* activity as one test for each marking period. This activity is a great way to build ownership and get the students actively engaged in the classroom in a meaningful way!

The Ultimate Test Review

Teachers are always looking for ways to make test reviews more stimulating and motivating. This activity is fun for students, and it is a way to review student knowledge in their modality strengths. This review is popular with students because it appeals to auditory, visual, and kinesthetic learners.

Materials needed

Teachers will need to provide a review sheet for each student. Put together a sheet of questions and a sheet of answers. The strips should be numbered independently of each other so that the first question or answer on each strip should be "number one." Next, cut the question sheet up into strips. Then, cut the answer sheet into strips. Each strip should contain a few questions or answers. Each student will receive a strip of paper. Some of the strips will have questions, and some of the strips will have answers.

Running the activity

As the students enter the room, each student receives one of the strips of paper that has been prepared from the question and answer sheets. Tell the students that they each have a sheet that either has a list of questions or a list of answers on it.

In a moment, they will hear some music. When the teacher turns the music on, the students will exchange sheets of paper as quickly as they possible. Leave the music on until sheets have been exchanged several times. Let the students know that when the music stops, each student must find the person that matches his or her number one question or answer.

Begin with number one on each strip of paper. If a student has a question, then he or she must find the student who has the answer for that question. If a student has an answer strip of paper, then he or she will look for the student who has the question for that answer.

Tell the students to feel free to help each other find the person that matches with their number one question or answer. When everyone has matched up with his or her number ones, read one of the number one questions out loud, and ask which student has that question. Then ask the student with the question to read it again to the class, and ask the student with the answer to read the answer out loud. Ask the class if everyone agrees on the answer with the question. If students agree, read another one of the number one questions to find out which pair of students has that question and the answer.

Again, ask the students to read their questions and answers out loud and check to see if the class agrees with the match.

When finished with all of the number one questions and answers, turn on the music again, and have the students switch slips as quickly as they can. Again, leave the music on for about a 5 count or until the students have switched slips of paper several times. When the music stops ask the students to look at their number two questions and answers. Now they must match up the number two questions with the correct number two answers.

Processing the activity

This is a fabulous way for teachers to review with their students. It is non-threatening because students are encouraged to help each other as they pair off. No student is ever singled out or put on the spot. If one pair of students gives the wrong answer for a question that means another pair of students has the wrong answer for another one of the questions.

Questions to ask and points to ponder

How does this activity make a class more brain-compatible, safe, challenging, and fun all at the same time? The visual learners will see each of the questions. When they see one of the questions on the test they will also remember the face of the student that read that particular question. Then they will remember what the student said, which of course is the answer. The auditory learners will hear each one of the questions and answers read out loud. They will remember the voices of the students as they read the questions and answers during the review. Finally, the kinesthetic learners will have physically walked through the test. They will remember where they were standing, and where the students were standing when they read the questions and answers.

With this review process there is something for everyone. This review encourages the students to help each other and share information. The students feel empowered by activities that actively engage them and that address their various learning styles.

Estimation Jar

The **Estimation Jar** is a weekly activity that gives students the opportunity to practice estimating skills. Teachers need to be prepared each week because students will quickly remind the teacher if she forgets to display the jar.

Materials needed

Empty plastic jars of different shapes and sizes are needed; empty peanut butter jars work well. Simply stick them in the dishwasher, and they make perfect estimation jars.

Setting up the activity

Set up an area for the *Estimation Jar* activity. This activity works well as a weekly bulletin board area. If bulletin board space is limited, simply write "Estimation Jar" on a poster board and tape it to the wall. Locate a small table or cart to hold the estimation jar. Then make guessing slips and a container for the slips.

Fill the **Estimation Jar** with items. Candy is a popular choice; however, there are a variety of items to use. Some examples are beans, paper clips, thumbtacks, dry pasta, marbles, etc.

Running the activity

Students need to be clear on the rules of the **Estimation Jar**. A student must guess exactly to get all of the candy. If a student's guess is the closest, but not exact, she gets a handful. If more than one person's estimate is exactly correct, then those students split the contents of the jar. If no one is correct, but more than one student is the closest to the correct number, then each student would get a handful. Students also need to know that they may guess one time only Monday through Thursday. Winners are posted on Friday.

Processing the activity

On Friday, the teacher reveals the number of items in the *Estimation Jar* and posts the winners on the board. At this point, ask students to share strategies for estimating. They often have other experiences where they used estimating skills.

Questions to ask and points to ponder

This is by far the favorite working bulletin board in the room. If teachers are not able to have candy in the jar, use some of the alternatives listed above. The reward for the winners could be a free homework assignment, extra credit, etc. If using the *Estimation Jar* with candy, teachers may want to give the candy to the winner at lunch, after school, or have the student take the candy to her locker. This eliminates classmates asking the student for candy.

Test Your Thinker

For teachers who like to challenge their students, this is the activity they have been looking for! These stimulating thinkers add excitement to the day. Students are extremely interested in the activity and often take the problems home to share with their family members.

Materials needed

A *Thinker* sheet (see page 40) for each student.

Setting up the activity

Prepare enough copies of the *Thinker* sheet so that each student has his or her own sheet. Make sure there is an answer key ready when it is time to go over the answers with students (see page 41).

Running the activity

Pass out the *Thinker* sheet and have students keep it face down until they are told to begin. Tell students they will have about seven minutes to work on the sheet and then they will check the answers together as a class. They may skip around and do the problems that they know. If they are not sure of the answer, they are encouraged to make an educated guess.

Processing the activity

It is fun to go over the questions and answers together as a class. Ask different students to read the questions. Even though students have read the information, it is good for students to hear the question before they hear the answer. It is fascinating to see how students work out the problems. There are a variety of methods that work, and students are encouraged to share them.

Questions to ask and points to ponder

Students are interested in the *Thinker* questions. The problems are challenging and engaging. Students will request to do the *Thinker* activity often. Frequently, they want to keep the sheets to use them at home to challenge their family.

Test Your Thinker

Use your thinker to solve the thinker problems listed below.

1. You have two coins that total 55 cents, and one is not a nickel. What are the two coins?

_____

2. If there are twelve dollars in a dozen, then how many dimes are in a dozen?

_____

3. Which would you rather have, an old ten-dollar bill or a new one?

_____

4. Take five oranges from seven oranges and what do you have?

_____

5. How many months in our calendar have twenty-eight days?

_____

6. History Link: Do they have a fourth of July in England? What about Canada?

_____

7. There was a boy in a candy store in Chicago. He was 5' 11" tall and 38 inches around the waist. What did he weigh?

_____

8. Solve the code in this series. YYURYYUBYYURYY4ME

_____

9. A monkey ate one hundred bananas in five days, each day eating six more than on the previous day. How many bananas did the monkey eat on the first day?

_____

Test Your Thinker Answer Key

1. You have two coins that total 55 cents, and one is not a nickel. What are the two coins?
   A 50-cent piece and a nickel are the two coins. Yes, one is not a nickel—but the other one is!

2. If there are twelve dollars in a dozen, then how many dimes are in a dozen?
   There are twelve dimes in a dozen. There are twelve of anything in a dozen.

3. Which would you rather have, an old ten-dollar bill or a new one?
   You would rather have an old ten-dollar bill than a new one-dollar bill.

4. Take five oranges from seven oranges and what do you have?
   You have five oranges (that is what you took).

5. How many months in our calendar have twenty-eight days?
   All months have 28 days.

6. History Link: Do they have a fourth of July in England? What about Canada?
   Yes—there is a fourth of July in England and Canada, they just don't celebrate Independence Day then. They also have a 5th, 6th, etc. of July.

7. There was a boy in a candy store in Chicago. He was 5' 11" tall and 38 inches around the waist. What did he weigh?
   He weighed CANDY!

8. Solve the code in this series. YYURYYUBYYURYY4ME
   Too wise you are, too wise you be, too wise you are, too wise for me!

9. A monkey ate one hundred bananas in five days, each day eating six more than on the previous day. How many bananas did the monkey eat on the first day?
   Eight: (1st day–8, 2nd day–14, 3rd day–20, 4th day–26, 5th day–32; total = 100)

$$100 = \underline{(d)} + \underline{(d + 6)} + \underline{(d + 6 + 6)} + \underline{(d + 6 + 6 + 6)} + \underline{(d + 6 + 6 + 6 + 6)}$$
$$100 = \underline{(d + d + d + d + d)} + \underline{(6 + 6 + 6 + 6 + 6 + 6 + 6 + 6 + 6 + 6)}$$
$$100 = 5d + 60$$
$$5d + 60 = 100$$
$$5d = 40$$
$$d = 8$$

© *2002 by Incentive Publications, Inc., Nashville, TN*

Marker Boards

This is a powerful way to reinforce concepts or review for tests. This activity encourages a productive class period with interesting discussion and results.

Materials needed

Each student will need a small marker board, marker, and eraser. If mini marker boards are not available, use a small chalkboard, chalk, and eraser. If none of these are available, students may use scrap paper and a pencil.

Setting up the activity

Students will need to be divided into groups of three or four (refer to **Round 'Em Up** on page 29). Spread the groups throughout the room. Questions will need to be prepared prior to the review. Questions or problems should be assembled into groups of five. Five groups of five questions work well; however, the number of questions should be adjusted depending on the time available.

For example, five questions might include:

1. What is the smallest whole number?

2. What is -4×-6?

3. Solve $-7 - -8 =$ ____

4. Solve $-92 + -45 =$ ____

5. In what quadrant would you find $(-2, 3)$?

Running the activity

Place the five questions on the overhead and allow the students ample time to work in groups. When one group is finished, give a one-minute warning. When checking the answers together, students will need to have their caps on the markers. If they miss a problem, they simply erase the incorrect answer. There is no need to remove the marker caps while the class is checking answers.

Some rules that work well are:

- Caps must be on markers while students are checking their answers. Any student who removes his cap is out for that round.

- All group members must have the same answers.

- The group(s) with the most correct answers for each round will obtain a point.

Points are awarded after each round of five questions. The group(s) with the most correct answers will get a point. A teacher may decide to offer extra credit for the winning group(s), a treat, or nothing at all. The game in itself is fun for students.

Processing the activity

The groups work together to solve problems and arrive at conclusions. Teachers find that there is a great deal of discussion during *Marker Boards*.

Questions to ask and points to ponder

Checking answers is a great time to reinforce concepts. Students have written an answer on the board and are intensely listening to hear the correct answer. Many students want an explanation if their answer is incorrect.

Marker boards create a situation where all students may write on the board. A word of advice: Having the same color markers for everyone saves a great deal of hassle.

Like-O

The *Like-O* game allows students an opportunity to know their classmates better. Students become familiar with the names of each person and a "like" or favorite thing associated with a specific student.

Materials needed

Each student will need a *Like-O* sheet (see page 45) and colored chips to use for place markers. The teacher will need a small slip of paper for every student or a class list cut into strips.

Setting up the activity

The teacher will need to ask each student to indicate his or her favorite food. The teacher should write this information on the board. Students will randomly fill in their *Like-O* board with the names and corresponding foods of particular students.

Running the activity

The teacher will need to write the name and food of each student on a small slip of paper. A class list could be cut into strips prior to the activity; then fill in the favorite food of each student. Place the small pieces of paper into a jar to use later for the drawing. When students have completed their boards, pull out one small piece of paper at a time and state the student's name and favorite food. The winner is whoever first has five answers in a row or diagonally.

Processing the activity

Students are able to share information about themselves with other students. This is an excellent activity for helping students learn about one another.

Questions to ask and points to ponder

Like-O can be used as a curriculum activity. Instead of writing a student's name, the class writes a word in each box. The words are selected from a word bank on the board. The definitions can be written in below the word. This activity will take a little longer; allow time to fill in the definitions. Another variation of the *Like-O* game is to use a favorite hobby in place of a favorite food. There are many variations—imagination is the key!

LIKE-O

_____ *Name* _____ *Favorite Food*	_____ *Name* _____ *Favorite Food*	_____ *Name* _____ *Favorite Food*	_____ *Name* _____ *Favorite Food*	_____ *Name* _____ *Favorite Food*
_____ *Name* _____ *Favorite Food*	_____ *Name* _____ *Favorite Food*	_____ *Name* _____ *Favorite Food*	_____ *Name* _____ *Favorite Food*	_____ *Name* _____ *Favorite Food*
_____ *Name* _____ *Favorite Food*	_____ *Name* _____ *Favorite Food*	_____ *Name* _____ *Favorite Food*	_____ *Name* _____ *Favorite Food*	_____ *Name* _____ *Favorite Food*
_____ *Name* _____ *Favorite Food*	_____ *Name* _____ *Favorite Food*	_____ *Name* _____ *Favorite Food*	_____ *Name* _____ *Favorite Food*	_____ *Name* _____ *Favorite Food*
_____ *Name* _____ *Favorite Food*	_____ *Name* _____ *Favorite Food*	_____ *Name* _____ *Favorite Food*	_____ *Name* _____ *Favorite Food*	_____ *Name* _____ *Favorite Food*

Brain Benders

Brain Benders are a fun way to challenge the mind. They may be used as a warm-up in class or as an extra credit assignment.

Materials needed

A *Brain Benders* sheet (see page 47).

Setting up the activity

When using the sheets as a group assignment, extra credit, or homework, make a copy for each student. If using them as a warm-up exercise, make a transparency of the *Brain Benders* sheet on page 45.

Running the activity

First, the teacher decides how to run **Brain Benders**. If **Brain Benders** is used for group work, give the students a specific amount of time to work together to solve the problems. If it is for extra credit, determine a due date for the optional assignment. If it is assigned as homework, set a due date and collect the work.

If using **Brain Benders** as a warm-up, make a transparency of the *Brain Benders* sheet and show one **Brain Bender** at a time. Allow students to guess at the **Brain Benders**. Enlarge the sheet so that all students may see it clearly.

Processing the activity

It is rewarding to see how creative students can become during this exercise. They often come up with alternative answers that make sense. This is a good way to emphasize how people see things differently. Sometimes we must change our line of thinking or look from another angle, and it becomes simple to find a solution. Students enjoy sharing real life examples of looking at things from another perspective.

Questions to ask and points to ponder

Students really enjoy **Brain Benders**. Have students make-up their own **Brain Benders** for other students to solve. Parents have fun with this activity as well. Frequently, teachers receive more ideas from parents who have done similar activities at work.

Answers:

1. Long underwear
2. A gross injustice
3. Unfinished symphony
4. Up in arms
5. Backward glance
6. Repeating decimal
7. Reading between the lines
8. A little light on the subject
9. Working overtime
10. 3 degrees below zero
11. Just between you and me
12. Touchdown
13. Crossroads
14. Scrambled eggs
15. It's a small world after all!

1 WEAR ——— LONG	**2** jus144tice	**3** symphon
4 allPrms	**5** ecnalg	**6** decimal decimal decimal
7 R|E|A|D	**8** light subject	**9** working time
10 0 ——— B.S. M.B.A. Ph.D.	**11** YOU JUST ME	**12** T O U C H
13 r r o a d a d	**14** G G S E	**15** ALL / WORLD

Perplexing People

Perplexing People is ideal for a "working" bulletin board; however, it may also be used as an assignment or as an extra credit area in the classroom.

Materials needed

Choose an area in the classroom to display the information; a bulletin board works well. Information is needed for each person, as well as guessing slips and a box or envelope for the slips.

Setting up the activity

Decorating the bulletin board is a nice idea. Try arranging a border and a title, such as *Perplexing People*. Or be more specific to the class content such as *Magnificent Mathematicians, Sensational Scientists, Powerful Poets,* and so on.

Running the activity

Tell students that each day there will be a clue up on the *Perplexing People* board. They may only guess once, and guesses are allowed Monday through Thursday. Students will soon discover that their odds are better if they wait to guess, since one clue will be added each day.

Processing the activity

On Friday, post the student winners, and post the answer. Students frequently share who they thought it was or how they arrived at their conclusion.

Questions to ask and points to ponder

Generally students will need to go beyond the classroom to figure out the solution to *Perplexing People*. It is a good idea to let the media center specialist know what the students are researching.

This activity may be used in any subject area. Teachers may use explorers, mathematicians, scientists, authors, writers, mythology, Presidents, heroes, and so on! The following pages share some ideas to get teachers started. Information for clues is available online, in encyclopedias, and in books.

Answers:

Magnificent Mathematician—Isaac Newton
Powerful Poets—Emily Dickinson
Sensational Scientists—Albert Einstein
Mysterious Mythology—Zeus

Magnificent Mathematicians
Who Am I?

Clues:

(Day 1) I entered Cambridge University in 1661. At that point I had not even read a math book. Within eight years, I mastered the subject and became a professor at that university.

(Day 2) Yes, I did it! I invented calculus.

(Day 3) I demonstrated that the law of gravity works throughout the universe.

(Day 4) I discovered that white light is composed of all the colors of the spectrum.

Powerful Poets
Who Am I?

Clues:

(Day 1) I was born in 1830 in Massachusetts.

(Day 2) I would not allow my poems to be published. While I was alive only three or four of my poems were printed.

(Day 3) It is true that people have been puzzled by my poetry, but people do agree that I was one of the greatest American poets.

(Day 4) I am a female.

Sensational Scientists
Who Am I?

Clues:

(Day 1)   More than likely I am best remembered for my theory of relativity.

(Day 2)   In 1921, I received the Nobel Prize in physics.

(Day 3)   I helped develop the quantum theory along with Planch, Heisenberg, and Schrodinger.

(Day 4)   My formula is $E = mc^2$

Mysterious Mythology
Who Am I?

Clues:

(Day 1)   My brother is Poseidon.

(Day 2)   My son is Hercules.

(Day 3)   My symbol is a thunderbolt.

(Day 4)   I am all-powerful and referred to as King of the Gods.

A Stick-Up KWL

This is a way for students to recall prior knowledge, link it to what they would like to know, and finally, list what they have learned.

Materials needed

Three different colors of self-stick notes and some chart paper are needed.

Setting up the activity

Students will need to be in groups for this activity; groups of three work best.

Running the activity

Before passing out any materials, demonstrate the ideas for students. Have students think of everything they can about cockroaches. As a demonstration, write these down either on the board or on self-stick notes. After students have exhausted all possibilities, ask them if there is anything they would like to know about cockroaches. Once they have given input, tell them a few facts about cockroaches. Some facts about cockroaches are . . .

They can live a month without food.

They can live a week without water.

They can hold their breath for forty minutes.

They can live nine days without their heads.

Once students have had a good laugh, ask them to write anything new that they learned. Do not worry if all the students' questions are not answered. This is a good opportunity to list resources for information, such as the library, Internet, books, encyclopedias, etc.

Tell students they are going to be using self-stick notes today to do a similar assignment. Select a topic in the class content for the activity. Some ideas are a state, a country, a continent, a kingdom, periodic table, nouns, fractions, and so on.

Ask students to list everything they can think of about the subject on the first color self-stick note. Have them stick the notes on a big sheet of poster board. At this point, discuss what the students feel they know about a topic, or teachers may choose to continue with the activity and discuss after the next step. After the first step, ask students what they want to learn about the subject. This is where they use the second color self-stick note.

When they are finished with step two, they stick the self-stick notes on the chart paper. Most teachers find it useful for students to discuss after they have formulated questions; however, teachers may choose to process at the end of the entire activity. At this point, choose to either read the class some information about the subject or pass out an information sheet on the subject. After students have processed this information, ask them to think of new information they have gathered and to write it on the third color self-stick notes.

Processing the activity

The students are more than willing to share what they know about the chosen topic, what they want to know, and finally, what they have learned. Process after each of the three parts of the activity. This breaks up the activity a little bit and adds to the discussion.

Questions to ask and points to ponder

This activity uses the reading strategy **KWL**. What do I **KNOW**? What do I **WANT** to know? What have I **LEARNED**? Many students have followed KWL routinely and are often ready for something new.

Instead of telling the kids **KWL**, ask them to list everything they can think of about the subject. After that step, ask them if they have any questions about the subject. Finally, have them think of new information they have gathered.

If there is a limited supply of self-stick notes, you can have students list the information on chart paper. If needed, use regular paper, but the self-stick notes add a new twist.

Check Please

Check Please is a method of working together and offering input. This activity proves that students delight in working with others.

Materials needed

Students need a sheet of problems to work on with their partners. Give one sheet to each group of two.

Setting up the activity

It is easy to set up this activity. The only pre-class work involved includes preparing questions or problems. Group the class into pairs. Set two pairs by each other so they are in a group of four.

Running the activity

The first partner will work problem one; then partner two will check the work and offer suggestions, if needed, and praise. Partner two works the next problem, and partner one checks the work, offering suggestions and praise. The group of four discusses each other's work and checks their answers within the group. The team offers suggestions, if needed. If the team cannot reach agreement on an answer, they all raise their hands, and the teacher assists.

Processing the activity

Students process the information within their pair and group of four. They should share and discuss information and correct answers if needed. This activity leads students toward becoming self-directed learners.

Questions to ask and points to ponder

Check Please allows students to work on class information and to discuss alternative methods to solving a problem. A good idea is to have a check mark at the end of each set of problems. This is a reminder to check with the other pair in the group. The check can either be circled or crossed off when complete. A sample set of problems is provided below. Teachers will want to use more than two problems, but this is an example to demonstrate.

Person one should solve the first problem. When person one is finished, person two will check the answer. Person two will offer suggestions, if needed.

Then person two will solve the second problem. When person two is finished, person one will check. Person one will offer suggestions, if needed.

$$\begin{array}{ll}
1.) \quad 245 & \qquad 2.) \quad 327 \\
\underline{\times\ 76} & \qquad \underline{\times\ 89}
\end{array}$$

When students are finished with both problems, they should check the answers with their group.

Corner Move

Corner Move can be used as a team building activity. *Corner Move* allows students to learn about their classmates. Use this activity as a "get to know you" exercise or with a content focus.

Materials needed

Four sheets of paper with different topics written on each sheet and chart paper (optional).

Setting up the activity

Select four different aspects of a topic. Assign one part to each corner of the room. Post the sheets with the topic marked clearly on each paper. Perhaps include an illustration to add visual appeal to the signs.

Running the activity

Students select one of the choices and then move to the corner of the room they have selected. Students must come up with a reason or two for why they selected that topic. Each section shares why its area was selected. One option is to group students together in each section or to take a student from each section to put in a group. Choose pairs from the groups.

If the corners are an academic area or discussion, choose to continue an activity after they are in the groups that relates to that topic. The corners could range from areas of the world to how students feel about specific amendments.

When using *Corner Move* for an academic activity, teachers may decide to have students list responses to questions on chart paper. If the groups are too large, use smaller groups or pairs for discussion.

Processing the activity

Students are willing to share why they selected the area they did. They will also share information on why they agree with a point or disagree with a point. *Corner Move* is a great way to actively involve the students and generate an interesting discussion.

Questions to ask and points to ponder

Require students to write their choice on a scrap piece of paper before they move. This strategy helps to eliminate the tendency for students to follow their friends to a certain corner of the room.

A variation of **Corner Move** involves designating a spot in the center of the room to which students may move if they do not agree with any of the four choices.

Sample activity:

Reproduce and hang one of the signs from page 56 in each corner of the room.
Have students select the vacation destination of their choice.

After the students are in the corners, split them up into small groups or pairs. Have them answer the questions below within their groups or pairs.

1. Why did you select this destination for your vacation?

2. Why do you feel your selection is better than the other three?

3. Have you visited any of the destinations before?

Extra: Make a poster advertising your chosen location.

Get in Shape

This activity may be used as a daily unit or for test review. *Get in Shape* will help reinforce concepts taught in class. This is a fun way to involve all the students and their different learning styles.

Materials needed

Heavy paper, cardstock, or poster board is required for this activity. Heavy copy machine paper can be used, so teachers may draw one shape and copy the rest. Three different colors of paper are needed, one color for each shape. A set of cards will include one square, one circle, and one triangle. Since each group of three students will use one set of cards, teachers need to determine how many sets are needed for the class. For example, if there are twenty four students in a class, there will be eight sets of students, so make eight sets of cards.

For each shape there will be two numbers; one will be on the front and the other on the back. So, on the front of the square will be the number 1, on the front of the circle will be the number 2, and on the front of the triangle, number 3. Likewise, on the back of the square will be the number 4, on the back of the circle will be the number 5, and on the back of the triangle will be the number 6.

Teachers will also need to make up six possible answers for each question. Use transparencies and place the choices on the overhead projector.

Setting up the activity

Arrange students into groups of three. Each group will need a set of shape cards. Be sure to make the shape cards prior to running the activity. The beauty of this activity is that once you have made the sets of cards, you may use them again and again.

Running the activity

Explain to students that they will be divided into groups of three and that each person will have a different shape card. There will be a number on the front and back of their cards. Since students often see the numbers 1, 2, and 3 along with three shapes and assume that there are only three choices, explain to them that in reality there are six choices since the front and back of the cards are used.

When students are in groups of three, direct one student to come up to the teacher and get a set of shape cards. The student will keep one card and give each student in his group a card.

There will be a series of questions with six possible answers. Once students hear the questions and see the possible answers on the overhead, give them time to discuss the choices and come to a conclusion on what they feel is the best possible answer. The teacher needs to have a signal such as a small buzzer, horn, or a count down to end the time period for conclusions.

Example:

The teacher asks the question, "Who was the sixteenth President of the United States?"
Then the teacher shows the possible answers on the overhead.

1. Herbert Hoover
2. Woodrow Wilson
3. Robert Kennedy
4. Abraham Lincoln
5. Dwight Eisenhower
6. Franklin Roosevelt

Allow students to discuss the choices within their groups. After some discussion, give a signal, at which time each group holds up the shape card that they feel holds the correct answer. In this example the answer was #4, which would be the square card with #4 facing the teacher.

Processing the activity

This is a fun way to reinforce concepts in the classroom. Students enjoy working with groups, holding up the cards, and seeing how many they answer correctly. Hold a brief discussion after each question. In the problem above, a good discussion starter would be, "What choice could have been quickly eliminated?" The answer would be Robert Kennedy, since he was never president. Often, there are obvious choices to eliminate on tests and assignments.

Questions to ask and points to ponder

Shape cards appeal to different types of learners. Shape cards encourage students to help each other, discuss ideas, and share information. Actively engaging students is extremely motivating. The shape card activity is a powerful tool to use in the classroom.

Equation Frustration

Equation Frustration requires some concentration and mental quickness. Students are asked to "decipher" the equations.

26 = abc's

Materials needed

Each student will need an *Equation Frustration* sheet (see page 60) and a pencil.

Setting up the activity

This activity is easy to set up. Simply make copies of **Equation Frustration** for all of your students.

Running the activity

It is a good idea to write an example on the board to solve with the students before beginning the activity. An example might be, "7 = D. in a W." The answer is *seven days in a week.*

There are different ways to use this information. Ask students to work in pairs, small groups, or on their own. This is also an excellent extra credit take-home assignment.

Processing the activity

It is helpful to go over the answers with students (see page 61 for answers). Things that seem so difficult to them are quickly understood and resolved.

Questions to ask and points to ponder

This activity may be used as a warm-up in class. Simply write one or two of the equations on the overhead projector or board and have students either guess aloud at the answer or write a guess on their papers or in their notebooks. Students often enjoy making up their own equations.

Equation Frustration Worksheet

Directions: Each problem is an equation that can be solved by substituting the appropriate words for the letters. Good luck!

1. 4 L.C. = G.L. _____

2. 3 = F. in 1 Y. _____

3. 1066 = Y. of B. of H. _____

4. N. + V. + P. + A. + A. + C. + P. + I. = P. of S. _____

_____

5. 26 = L. of A. _____

6. 1000 = W. that a P. is W. _____

7. S. + H. of R. = U.S.C. _____

8. 24 = H. in a D. _____

9. T. = L. S. State _____

10. N. E. states = M. + M. + N. H. + V. + C. + R. I. _____

_____

11. 365 = D. in a Y. _____

12. 60 M. = 1 H. _____

13. 12 = S. of the Z. _____

14. 54 = C. in the D. (with the J.) _____

15. 9 = P. in the S.S. _____

16. 5 = D. in a Z.C. _____

17. 13 = S. on the A.F. _____

18. 29 = D. in F. in a L.Y. _____

19. 32 = D. F. at which W. F. _____

20. 88 = P.K. _____

21. 7 = W. of the W. _____

22. 12 = M. in a Y. _____

Fire Up For Learning

Answers for Equation Frustration

1. 4 L.C. = G.L	*(Four-leaf clover = good luck)*
2. 3 = F. in 1 Y.	*(3 = feet in a yard)*
3. 1066 = Y. of B. of H.	*(1066 = year of Battle of Hastings)*
4. N. + V. + P. + A. + A. + C. + P. + I. = P. of S.	*(Nouns, Verbs, Pronouns, Adjectives, Adverbs, Conjunctions, Prepositions, Interjections = Parts of Speech)*
5. 26 = L. of A.	*(26 = letters of the alphabet)*
6. 1000 = W. that a P. is W	*(A thousand = words that a picture is worth)*
7. S. + H. of R. = U.S.C.	*(Senate and House of Representatives = United States Congress)*
8. 24 = H. in a D.	*(24 = hours in a day)*
9. T. = L. S. State	*(Texas = Lone Star state)*
10. N. E. states = M. + M. + N. H. + V. + C. + R. I.	*(New England states = Maine, Massachusetts, New Hampshire, Vermont, Connecticut, Rhode Island)*
11. 365 = D. in a Y.	*(365 = days in a year)*
12. 60 = M. in 1 H.	*(60 = minutes in 1 hour)*
13. 12 = S. of the Z.	*(12 = signs of the zodiac)*
14. 54 = C. in the D. (with the J.)	*(54 = cards in a deck with the jokers)*
15. 9 = P. in the S. S.	*(9 = planets in the solar system)*
16. 5 = D. in a Z. C.	*(5 = digits in a zip code)*
17. 13 = S. on the A. F.	*(13 = stripes on the American flag)*
18. 29 = D. in F. in a L.Y.	*(29 = days in February in a Leap Year)*
19. 32 = D. F. at which W. F.	*(32 = degrees Fahrenheit at which temperature water freezes)*
20. 88 = P. K.	*(88 = keys on a piano)*
21. 7 = W. of the W.	*(7 = wonders of the world)*
22. 12 = M. in a Y.	*(12 = months in a year)*

Think—Pair—Share It!

Think-Pair-Share It works well for teachers and students; they learn a great deal from the process. Students are able to share their responses and discuss information.

Materials needed

A problem or question from the teacher.

Setting up the activity

It is easy to set up this activity. Just have questions or problems prepared and group the class into pairs.

Running the activity

Ask a question or give a problem to the students and have them think about the solution. After students have thought about their response, pair students up to discuss their ideas. Once they have discussed their answers, pair them up with another group to share. After the four have shared information, have the class share the ideas, solutions, and possibilities.

Processing the activity

Students are constantly processing the information. They process with their partner, with their group, and then with the class. Students will often see that there are many ways to arrive at an answer.

Questions to ask and points to ponder

If the class does not have an even number of students, the teacher may decide to pair up with a student or have one group of three. When a teacher pairs up with a student, it provides a good opportunity to have some one-on-one attention with a student.

Run-Around

This is a fantastic game for emphasizing concepts, reviewing topics, and reinforcing curriculum. Students truly enjoy this activity. They will often come back to that class years later and inquire about the game.

Dorothy's former middle school teacher, Mr. Haase, developed a form of this game that is still a vivid memory for her. Dorothy's older brother had the same teacher and still remembers the game and final round. Mr. Haase is definitely a master teacher who still has an impact on students today through the dedication of many former students who are now educators.

Materials needed

This activity requires scorecards, two different colors of poster board for the score cards, a piece of white poster board for each class, masking tape, a marker, and an area in which to play the game.

Setting up the activity

Students should be organized into groups of three for the game. Let students select their own groups. When students are in groups of three, they are to agree upon an appropriate group name.

The teacher will then prepare scorecards. Cut 4" x 4" squares from the colored poster board. Yellow and orange poster board works well. Write a '3' on each orange square and a '1' on each yellow square. Make approximately forty-five 3-point cards and ten 1-point cards. See sample below.

The white poster board will need to be sectioned into pieces with a marker to form a chart. Draw horizontal lines about an inch apart. Write the team names on the left side of the poster board, then draw vertical lines about two inches apart. This chart will be used by the teacher to record the team scores. See sample on page 64.

Sample scorecard

Sample chart

Three Musketeers										
Smarties										
The Butterflies										
Survivors										
The Terminators										
High Flyers										
Sunshine										

First, create a game area on the floor of the classroom. Use masking tape to create three sections with two strips of tape. Use the tape to make the sections and put the numbers 1, 2, and 3 in separate sections.

Next, prepare nine questions from the class content area and six questions from current events. Each question will need three multiple-choice answers.

Running the activity

Play this game once a week every Friday for about eight or nine weeks. It takes about twenty minutes to go through the questions and total the scores. Allow more than twenty minutes the first time playing the game. Students will sit with their group during the game. Students need to determine the order of their rotation. Allow only one student from each group in the play area during a question. If a class has twenty-four students, eight will be in the play area for each question. Each student will be in the play area five times. Players are not allowed to help teammates when in the play area.

When the first players from each group are in the play area, read the first question. Example: What is the smallest whole number?

        1) –1   2) 0   3) 1

Read the question only two times. Give students five seconds to reach the right answer (section on the floor). Count aloud so students are aware of the time frame, "5-4-3-2-1-STOP." Be strict with your rule on STOP—students must be in a section. If students are in between sections when the teacher says "STOP," they are out for that round. Continue this process with all fifteen questions.

Scoring

There are three ways to obtain points. If a student is on the correct answer with other students, each student receives a 3-point card. If a student is alone on the wrong answer, she receives a 1-point card for taking a risk. If a student is alone on the correct answer, he receives a Grand Slam—a 3-point card and a 1-point card (a total of four points).

Correct — on the right answer with other people . . . . 3-point card

Risk Taker — alone on the wrong answer . . . . 1-point card

Grand Slam — alone on the right answer . . . . 3-point card and 1-point card

Processing the activity

At the end of the game (after question 15) have one student from each group bring up their group's scorecards to the teacher. Total the points and record the information on the white poster board. Each week total the points; at the end of the 9 weeks there will be a classroom winner. If a teacher has more than one class, have a *Run-Around Finale* with the champs from each class. The finale round will consist of twenty-one questions (nine content-based, six current events, and six from other areas *or* fifteen content-based and six current events questions).

Questions to ask and points to ponder

The overall champions (3 students) win a big reward, such as lunch out with the teacher, or a local field trip with the teacher. The top classroom teams could have an appropriate reward for making the finals (candy bar, pop, etc.). If all students watch the finale, a teacher may opt to offer a small reward for the class that has the overall winning team. The reward could be a piece of candy, extra credit, a pencil, etc. This encourages students to cheer and support their classmates. Teachers may also decide to recognize the high-scoring team each week with a small reward such as a piece of candy, sticker, pencil, extra credit, and so on.

Be sure to use the local news, the national news, and the newspaper for obtaining weekly sports and current events. The content questions can be prepared in advance. Most teachers use three sports and three current events from the week their class is going to play.

The *Run-Around* concept allows students to move around for five seconds, so that other students do not know where anyone will actually stop. For those teachers concerned about the noise level—never fear, the students take care of this issue. They do not want to miss the question, so they keep each other quiet during this time. Enjoy this activity, and think of the great teachers who have come before, like Mr. Haase.

Write Like Paul Harvey

Paul Harvey is a creative writer who generates curiosity and holds the attention of his readers. Students will find his stories fascinating while they learn some interesting information.

Materials needed

Obtain one or both of the Paul Harvey books. Paul Harvey's **The Rest of the Story** and **More of Paul Harvey's Rest of the Story** are both good titles to use.

When including the writing portion of this activity, find a list of people from the class subject area. For example, a math teacher will need a list of mathematicians; a science teacher will need a list of scientists, and so on.

Setting up the activity

Decide which stories to read prior to reading aloud to the students.

Running the activity

Read about two stories a week to the students. Remember the stories are brief and are fun to read. A weekly story is also a good idea, since the student can plan on hearing **The Rest of the Story** every Friday or another convenient day of the week.

Read one story at a time and allow students to guess who the person is or what the event might be at the end of the story. When students understand how Paul Harvey writes, throw in a writing assignment. Give each student the name of a person who is connected to the classroom's content area.

Require each student to write a paper about that person in the Paul Harvey format … "Now You Know the Rest of the Story." Choose one student to read his or her story in class and allow the other students to guess who the person might be.

During the second semester, teachers may try another writing assignment. This time, students may select a person of their choice. It could be a famous person or even someone they know. Many students select one of their parents, which adds special meaning to the process. The last paragraph should state how their subject of the story uses the class's content in his or her own daily life.

Processing the activity

Students enjoy listening to the stories and guessing the identity of the person or event. They also enjoy the second writing activity since they select the person. They take ownership in the process and have fun doing it. Students learn an immense amount of information about people in history, events, famous people, and their own parents. Since students must find out how the person they selected uses school information in the real world, it is great tool to tie a subject area into everyday life.

Questions to ask and points to ponder

Some teachers choose to do only the second writing assignment, and that works well also. Other teachers have decided just to read the stories to the students. These teachers often try to find stories that relate to their area and use the stories to enhance their lesson.

There is also a video of Paul Harvey stories. An alternate option is to show this video once a week to your students.

Outside the Box

Outside the Box is a wonderful activity that adds enrichment and challenges the students. This activity works well if used on a weekly basis throughout the year, but it may also be used for a marking period.

Materials needed

Teachers need a problem for each week that they decide to implement **Outside the Box** and response forms for student responses.

Setting up the activity

A bulletin board works great for **Outside the Box**. Set up an area in the classroom for the problem, last week's solution, and the names of the winners. Next, create a shoebox covered in paper or a manila envelope with a slice in the front. Students insert their solutions in the shoebox or envelope. Students will need slips of paper to record the information. Try using colorful paper for the problem, or type the problem and color a border. It is a good idea to laminate the problems when time is invested in constructing them.

Running the activity

The bulletin board or area in the classroom should be set up before explaining **Outside the Box** to students. Tell students that the problem will be posted Monday through Thursday and winners will be posted on Friday. Students may make only one guess.

Processing the activity

On Friday, share the names of winners (and the answer) with students. Allow the winner(s) to demonstrate how she or he solved the problem. There may be times when there are many winners and times when there are no winners.

Questions to ask and points to ponder

Students begin to look at problems differently and will often connect the *Outside the Box* problem to other curriculum areas.

Students are creative and often have interesting methods for solving the problems. Offer extra credit or candy for the winners. More than likely, students go for the candy, if candy is allowed.

The following pages provide enough *Outside the Box* problems for a nine-week marking period. Photocopy these for classroom use and paste them on colorful paper. Feel free to add some color for visual appeal. Remember, it is also a good idea is to laminate the cards for future use.

Sample Response Form

Outside the Box

Name: _____

Solution: _____

Answers

_____

_____

_____

_____

_____

_____

_____

_____

_____

OUTSIDE THE BOX Problems

#1

? ? ? ? ?

Where should the number 9 be placed to complete the sequence below?

8, 5, 4, 1, 7, 6, 3, 2

ANSWER: Between the 4 and the 1; the numbers are in alphabetical order

#2

? ? ? ? ?

John faces 50 steps.
The faster he climbs one step at a time,
the more steps he must take to get to the top!
Why?

ANSWER: John is facing an escalator. He is going upward on an escalator.

#3

? ? ? ? ?

A bottle and a cork cost $2.20.
If the bottle costs $2.00 more than the cork,
how much does the cork cost?

ANSWER: 10 cents; the difference must be $2.00 , so $2.10 — $ .10 = $2.00

#4

? ? ? ? ?

Can you find
1,000
100
and 10
hiding in the sentence below? Explain!

My brother Cam went out the EXIT.

#5

? ? ? ? ?

Your mom gave you 3 pills

and said to take 1 every $\frac{1}{2}$ hour.

How long will the pills last?

#6

? ? ? ? ?

Mr. and Mrs. Thompson have five children.
Half are boys.
How is this possible?

ANSWER: All the children are boys.

#7

? ? ? ? ?

If it takes 5 seagulls five minutes to catch five fish,
how long would it take 50 seagulls to catch fifty fish?

ANSWER: Five minutes

#8

? ? ? ? ?

Can you determine the two missing numbers to complete this numeric sequence?

_ 1 3 2 4 5 6 _ 11

ANSWER: 1 and 9 (you add 2 adjacent numbers and skip 1 — that is the total)

#9

? ? ? ? ?

Patti the Pet Lover has seven pets.

She has some cats and some dogs.

They got into the cracker jar.

Each dog ate five crackers and each cat ate four crackers.

Thirty-two crackers in total were gobbled up.

How many cats and how many dogs are there?

ANSWER: 4 dogs and 3 cats

Knot-ty Activities

Knot-ty activities involve a variety of knots of both the rope and human variety. These knots were never used by sailors or taught by the Boy Scouts, but they will be motivating and highly challenging. Students never knew that learning could be this much fun!

The Great Houdini

Teachers will be curious to see if their students can figure out how to get out of this one. If they can escape from their partner, they qualify for the Houdini award because even the great Houdini could not get out of this one (of course, there is no proof that Houdini ever even heard of this challenge, but most students think their teachers are old enough to have known him personally!).

Materials needed

Ropes with loops tied in each end are needed. Cotton clothesline cut into about 5-foot lengths works well Tie a small loop in each end just big enough for hands to fit through. After tying loops in each end, the ropes are about 3 1/2 to 4 feet long. This activity requires a set of these ropes for the classroom.

Setting up the activity

Begin by dividing the students into groups of four, or students may be organized into pairs. Make up a story about the one great escape that Harry Houdini himself never could figure out until, of course, a teacher helped him! Tell each group to send one person up to the teacher to get the materials for the activity, and give each group two ropes. Send the students back to their groups to await the instructions.

Running the activity

Two students in each group take one rope and lock themselves together by putting their hands through the end loops (see diagram 1 on page 77).

Now the idea is for the two students to get apart. The only rule is that the loops must stay on each student's wrists during the entire activity; they may not untie or cut the ropes.

The students must manipulate the ropes and themselves to get the ropes free. The ropes are long enough to encourage the students to try many different strategies. The students can get into some unusual positions as they step in, over, and through the ropes.

Groups of four are suggested for this activity because there are a variety of roles for the students to play. Some students prefer to watch, analyze, and provide suggestions for the two with the ropes. If everyone in the group would like having a rope and a partner they certainly may. Often the ones making the suggestions will get an idea, and they will request more ropes to try their theory. Soon the students will realize that they have two interlocking circles, and they cannot solve the problem by trying to step through the ropes in some way.

The Solution

Person A takes the left side of her rope and sticks it through the loop on Person B's left hand, going from palm to fingertips (be sure that the rope is guided through from between Person B's hands). Then, Person A pulls her rope through and slips the new loop up and over Person B's hand. At this point, if both people pull there hands apart, the ropes will "unlock!"

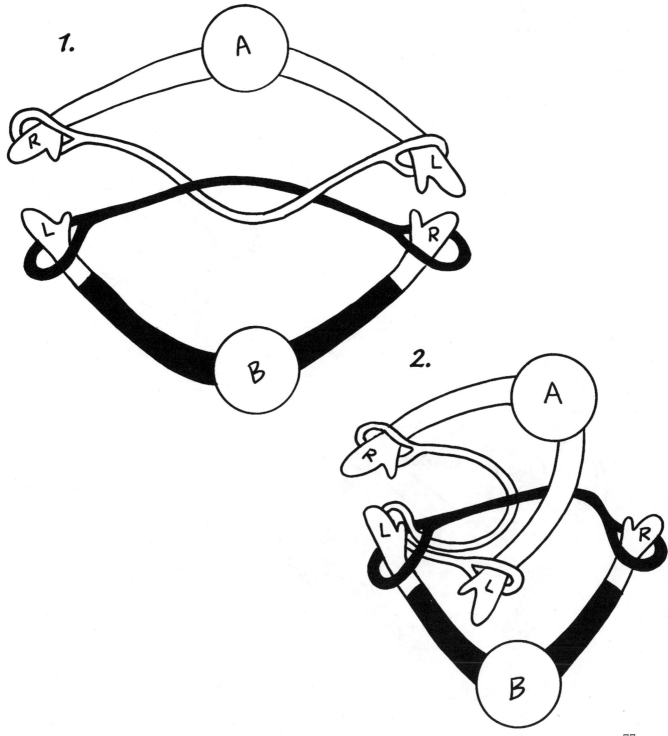

3.

4.

5.

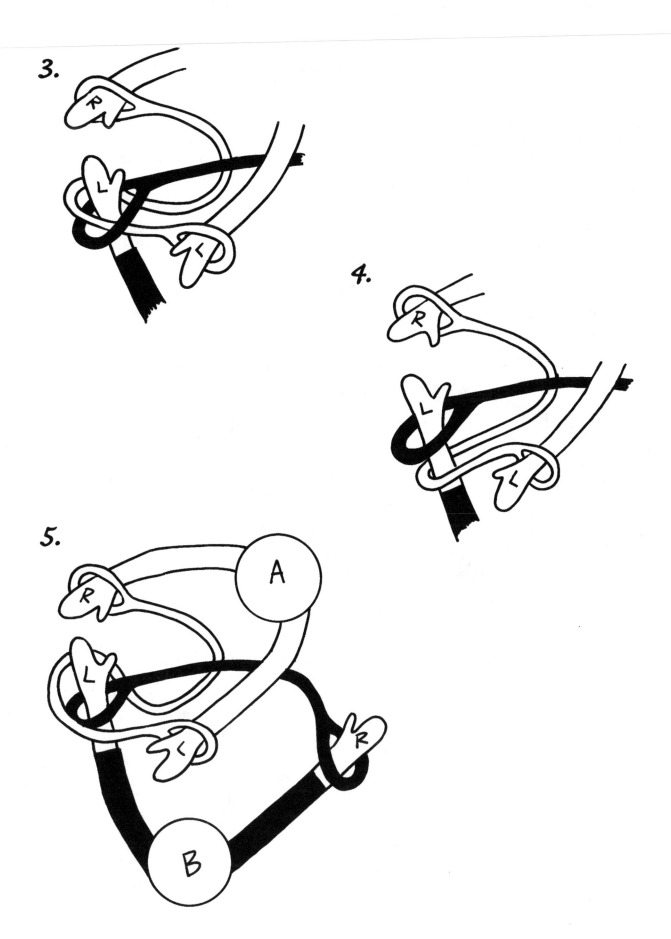

Processing the activity

One of the interesting things about this activity is that it is predicated on failure. Most of the students will not be able to do this one at first, if at all. The students will be captivated by this activity.

Questions to ask and points to ponder

The first question for the students is, "What did you have to do to solve this problem?" Lead the discussion to get into thinking out of the box. Also discuss brainstorming and using each other's ideas to look at the problem differently. Then relate thinking out of the box to schoolwork. Demonstrate how the same kind of thinking is required on some standardized tests. What may appear to be the most obvious solution is not always the right one, and students have to be able to look beyond the obvious.

Another point to ponder with the students is how the communication is developed throughout the activity. Listen to the students as they try to solve this one. The directions will become more specific as the activity continues. Talk with students about giving good directions and about how easy it can be to misunderstand something that someone has said. After all, if the speaker always knows exactly what he means, why doesn't everyone else?

The next question is, "How many different ways did you try to do this?" Discuss how frustrating it can be to not be able to do something. Often students in middle school do not handle frustration well. Talk about what happens when their homework does not work out the first time. Instead of quitting, they should do it again and again. It is normal if something does not work out right the first time. Students today are accustomed to instant gratification, and they need to learn that even greater satisfaction may come when overcoming more substantial obstacles.

Finally, teachers will love the facial and verbal expressions by students when the solution is revealed. There is always a loud "Ah, Hah," with a look of amazement and wonder. Make sure to point out how the students react and how much fun it is to find a solution. Be sure to encourage them to share other moments of discovery with each other.

Untangle the Tangle

Everyone has had experience with trying to untangle knots. It may have been with shoestrings, fishing line and tackle, a necklace, or cords for the computer or the entertainment center, but, regardless, this frustrating and challenging experience is familiar to most people.

Materials needed

A rope measuring fifty feet or longer. In a pinch, a 50-foot extension cord will do.

Setting up the activity

Tie several knots in the rope. Use just the standard overhand knot, and put at least four knots in the rope. The more knots, the longer it takes for the activity. Teachers generally use six and space them apart evenly. Then put the rope in the hallway, outside, or in some other area that will allow the rope to be stretched out on the ground.

Have students come where the rope is, and tell them that they all have to help pick up the rope. Tell them it does not matter which side of the rope they are on, but they must all be holding on to the rope. Then tell students that they are to hold the rope with one hand only when they decide where they are going to hold on. Students may use either hand, and they may not remove their hands until the activity is complete.

The knots that are tied in the rope will divide the group into a number of sections. The students in each section may slide the hand they are holding on with up and down the rope; however, when their hand reaches another member of the group or one of the knots, they must stop. They will each have one free hand. Tell them they may use their free hand any way they want to solve the problem, within the realm of respect and responsibility.

Just for fun, to change this activity for later use, try putting a blindfold on every other student.

Running the activity

Tell students that they must untie all of the knots without ever letting go of the rope. What they will soon discover is that they must loosen the knots one at a time to make the knots big enough for them to be able to step through. It usually starts out well organized by the students, but often begins to break down as they have to move more and more students through the knots. Then a pattern develops, and they see that they must work from the ends toward the middle.

Processing the activity

In the initial dialogue of the students, they will talk about "your" knot and "my" knot. They will say things like "You untie that knot, and we will untie this one," and so on. Soon they discover that they all have to step through the knots and that the knots go from "yours and mine" to become "our knots."

Questions to ask and points to ponder

Point out how the students assign the knots to different groups at first, and then ask how this had to change. Soon it becomes apparent that they must all work together to get all of the knots out of the rope. People in general are often quick to say things like, "That is her problem, that is not my problem."

A powerful point to emphasize to students is that if they are not part of the solution, then they are part of the problem! This can be a difficult concept for adults and even more so for middle school students. Students need to understand that as soon as they become aware of a problem, they have only two choices. They may become a part of the solution, or they will help perpetuate the problem. For example, some may never spread a rumor, but listening to a rumor gives it an audience and endorses it.

As mentioned earlier, change this activity and make it even more challenging by blindfolding every other student. The discussion will then lead to how the students that were not blindfolded had to help those who were. It is possible to talk about how students can focus on a problem and not the people involved. Here they focus on the rope and the knots, and it really does not matter who is blindfolded and who is not or who is on the other side of a knot.

Lend a Hand

Those that have ever been in a large crowd at a major event may have felt like they were part of a tangle of humanity; this activity will feel similar. This activity creates a knot using students. The task for the students will be to untangle the knot of bodies.

Materials needed

It is a good idea to use connectors for this activity. Connectors are short ropes with loops at each end. Use cotton clothesline and make each connector about a foot long. To do this, cut 2-3 foot lengths and tie loops in each end. The idea of connectors is to allow students to hold hands without actually holding hands. If two students each hold one end of a connector, they are connected as if they were holding hands, but they are about a foot apart. This allows for flexibility and eliminates all of the issues of holding hands, not the least of which include sweaty palms and personal space. Some teachers have used things like bandannas or their blindfolds for connectors. Feel free to use connectors any time an activity would call for the students to hold hands.

Setting up the activity

Begin the activity by arranging the students into groups of 8 or 10. Tell the groups to get into a tight, shoulder-to-shoulder circle. Have the students take someone else's right hand (or connector). They may take anyone's hand except the two people immediately beside them. Then they should raise their left hands and take someone else's left hand. Each student in the circle should be holding the right hand of one student and the left hand of a different student.

Running the activity

The task of the students now is to untangle the tangle of arms. By using the connectors, the students will be able to step back a little, have more room to work, and be better able to step over, around, and through each other to untangle the knot. With the connectors, they are also able to see the problem more clearly. The problem is solved when the knot is untied.

As the students untangle the knot, let them know that some of the students will end up facing out as they reform the circle. It is also possible that, as they untangle the original knot, they may actually form two (or three) new circles that may or may not be interlinked. A variation of the activity would be making a break in the circle before the students begin to untangle themselves, creating two loose ends. When the students untangle the knot, they will end up in a line.

Processing the activity

To solve this problem, the students have to look and communicate three-dimensionally as they try to move through the many layers of arms. Like learning a new computer game or playing chess, the students will have to pause often to contemplate their next move. Some students say it also looks like a dance as they all move together.

Questions to ask and points to ponder

The obvious question is, "What did you all have to do to solve this problem?" As the students talk about solving this problem, teachers will have the opportunity to make points about cooperation, communication, helping each other, focusing on a task, and, of course, patience and perseverance.

Ask the students to ponder why it can be so much fun to solve a problem like this. Then the question becomes, "How can we make your classwork like this?" Students often perceive classwork challenges as work, and these types of challenges as fun. Teachers need to listen closely as the students talk about this experience because the students will give teachers some great ideas for making their class more fun and interesting.

As Easy as Tying Your Shoe!

People, in general, feel that they explain things well and that it is frustrating to be misunderstood. This activity will test student communication skills to the limit.

One of the tasks anyone over the age of five takes for granted is tying the laces on his shoes. It is easy to forget how difficult it was to learn. After this activity, teachers and their students will never take tying their shoes for granted again, and they will have a better understanding of misunderstandings.

Materials needed

Each student will need a sheet of paper and a pen or pencil.

Setting up the activity

Set up this activity by having a short discussion about how easy it is to misunderstand someone.

Running the activity

Ask the students to imagine that they have just met an alien who has never seen a pair of shoes before. This alien wants to fit in; therefore, he will have to know how to tie his shoes. The students will not be there the first time he has to tie his shoelaces, so they will have to leave instructions for him. Challenge the students to write the instructions for tying the laces on a shoe. Our alien must be able to follow the written directions, and he must be able to tie his shoe laces.

Give the students at least fifteen minutes to accomplish this task, and then put the students into pairs. Have one student read his or her directions to the other student, and see if the student is able to tie his shoes. The student tying her shoes must follow the directions exactly and may not try to anticipate what the other student meant. The instructions must be followed exactly and literally. Then the students switch roles and try the other student's directions.

See if there are one or two brave souls willing to read their instructions out loud while the teacher tries to follow them for the whole class. The teacher can demonstrate what is meant by following directions exactly.

Not all students will have shoes with laces. Bring several pairs of old sneakers to share. Usually teachers are able to round up enough pairs of shoes, since only one shoe is needed per group.

Processing the activity

It is fun to see the wrinkled brows of the students as they try to write their instructions. It is even more entertaining to watch them try to follow each other's instructions. This is a great lesson for everyone, especially for middle level students.

Questions to ask and points to ponder

The first question is simply, "How did it go?" Direct the conversation as the students relate their trials and tribulations in trying to explain how to tie the shoe laces. Discuss how difficult it can be to explain a task to other people. What about when someone is sure he knows how to do something, but cannot explain it to someone else? Ask students if they have ever had this happen on a test. They thought they knew the material, but could not demonstrate that on the test.

The next point to ponder is the difficulty of listening without anticipating what the direction-giver will say next. Many of the students put their own words into the directions as they listened to the student giving the directions. Have the students talk about how a person sometimes hears what he or she wants to hear instead of what is actually said. Usually a great discussion follows as students share related stories of hearing what they wanted to hear.

Finally, for the brave, ask the students if a teacher has given them unclear instructions. Think about any time students have ever come into class and have said something like, "That homework assignment did not make any sense at all!"

Squaresville

Teachers may have to explain what **Squaresville** means to their students. And for those teachers too young to remember, ask one of the school's more experienced teachers! This activity takes being a square to a whole new level.

Materials needed

This activity requires one fifty-foot rope for the class and a blindfold for each student.

Setting up the activity

For this activity, students need a large open area. The cafeteria with some of the tables up or an outside area will work well. Take the rope, the bag of blindfolds, and the students to the area. Tell the students a story to set up the activity. Use the story on page 87, or make up one to use.

Running the activity

There are many ways to get the students into this activity. Good News/Bad News stories are especially good to set up this activity. Tell students that with every bit of good news, there is bad news, and with every bit of bad news, there is also good news. Then, start a story with either good news or bad news. If starting with good news, then the students are to ask loudly what the bad news is, and back and forth until the story is finished. The students really get into this activity with a good story. The following is our story, and we are sticking to it!

Example story

"Here is a good news/bad news story, and today we are going to start with the bad news."

Pause here and encourage the students to ask loudly, "What's the bad news?"

"The bad news is that there has just been a nuclear disaster. The Thompson Nuclear Facility has just exploded!"

Pause here, as the students ask loudly, "What's the good news?"

"The good news is that we knew it was going to happen, and we were able to successfully evacuate everyone from the facility before the explosion. So no one was injured by the explosion."

Pause, as the students ask loudly, "What's the bad news?" We'll bet you are beginning to see the pattern, so from here we will let you know when to pause, and you know that the students will be asking loudly for the next piece of news.

"The bad news is that you were all looking toward the facility when the explosion happened. The flash of the explosion was so bright that it has temporarily blinded you all."

Pause. Pass out the blindfolds, and have the students put them on.

"The good news is that while there is fallout coming our way, the rescue helicopters are on the way. The helicopters will be here in plenty of time to evacuate all of us to a safe distance."

Pause.

"The bad news is that there is a fog that has developed in our area. The fog has become so dense that the rescue helicopters will not be able to see us when they get here."

Pause.

"The good news is that we have the rescue rope here that was designed just for this rescue. This specially designed rescue rope is a bright neon color, which can be seen through a dense fog. In a moment, we are going to give one member of your group the rope. If you all find that person and take hold of the rope you will be saved. Only those of you holding on to the rope will be saved."

Pause.

"This is the last bit of news. After this news you may start. The bad news is that the helicopters need a perfect square to land in. You must all find the person with the rope, take hold of the rope, and form a perfect square with the rope. You must use all of the rope to make the largest square possible, and you must all be holding the rope before the helicopters can land. When you think that you have formed the largest square possible, let us know, and you will be able to take off your blindfolds. There is no more news. Go for it!"

Processing the Activity

It is so much fun to watch and listen to the students as they work their way through this one. There will be too many leaders, and not enough followers, and too many talkers, and not enough listeners. Often, one of the first things most groups do is number off hoping that they will be able to put an equal number of students on each side. Since there is only a one in four chance that the number will be divisible by four, the odds are that this strategy will not work. Even if the number is divisible by 4, getting the students evenly spaced, forming the corners, and getting the ends together are all difficult tasks.

Questions to ask and points to ponder

The first question to ask is, "What made this activity so difficult?" There will be many points to ponder as the students begin to discuss this activity. One thing the students will share is that there were so many students talking, it was difficult to know who to listen to. As with other activities, talk about how students choose to whom they listen. Another point to ponder would be, "If a student near you has a good idea that the group has not heard, do you have a responsibility to help get the group to listen to the idea?" This question certainly applies to every classroom.

The next point to ponder is how the leaders emerged as the activity progressed. The leadership roles usually change depending on whose idea the group is currently trying. Sometimes being a great leader means knowing when to follow.

This activity also allows students to work on communication skills. The students begin to understand how difficult it can be for a teacher to describe something or to get a point across. In this case, the blindfolds are the barriers to communication. One group had the great idea of folding the rope in half and then folding it in half again to get four equal sides. All but two of the students let go of the rope until it was folded. The student that had the idea asked two more students to take the corners and back up. Then the rest of the students walked up and took hold of the rope assuming that the rope was now in the shape of a square.

When the four students took the four corners and backed up, they actually had the ropes crisscrossing each other and formed a very nice Star of David instead of a square! The entire group was absolutely certain they had formed a square. Like the three blind men trying to describe an elephant, from the students' perspective, they were describing a square.

What someone thinks he heard is not always what was said, and what someone thinks she saw is not always exactly what was there. Then, ask students, "How can two people see the exact same incident, and yet tell very different stories about what happened?" Is it possible to tell the truth, explaining exactly what you saw, and yet not be accurate?

Of course, there are many points to ponder here, and teachers can decide which avenue to pursue. Other topics to discuss include the following: teamwork, cooperation, following directions, listening skills, and problem solving, just to name a few. This is an activity that lends itself to many academic and social situations while being fun and motivating as well.

Advisory Activities

The Plague

This activity will demonstrate why anything can spread from person to person quickly, even with limited contact. This activity is also great fun to demonstrate how rumors can spread quickly and why pyramid schemes look so attractive.

Materials needed

Provide one 3 x 5 card for each student. On one side write "infected" in red, and on the other side write "not infected" in another color, like blue. This activity can be done without the cards if there is not time to make some.

Setting up the activity

This is an activity that works with one class or the entire teaching team. It is most effective when a couple of classes get together and there are a few more students. **The Plague** is also a great staff activity. Tell the students that they will be testing the effects of a new biological weapon. It is a simple virus and does not sound very deadly because it can only be passed person to person. In other words, once a person has been infected, only those that come into contact with that person can become infected; however, it is always fatal. Even though it can only be passed one person at a time, this will be a test to see how fast a virus of this type might spread.

Running the activity

Give out the cards, and tell the students to hold their cards in front of them so that the blue side that reads "not infected" is showing. Then tell the students that their teacher has the virus, and pick one student to be the next to be infected. That student has to turn her card over to show that she is infected. Record on the board how many students are now infected. Then, ask that student to go to one other student and infect him or her by turning his card over. Again, record how many students are now infected.

Ask those two students to each pick one student to infect. The two students go to two non-infected students and infect them by turning their cards over. Then, record the number of students infected. After recording how many students are infected, ask all of the students that are infected to go out and infect one more student each. Even if the entire team is involved in the activity, everyone will be infected within 7 contacts, or 8 if it is an extremely large team.

Processing the activity

The students are always amazed at how fast everyone is infected with the virus. It starts out slowly and then picks up speed quickly. This activity is applicable to many situations. Try changing the cards to say "have heard the rumor" and "have not heard the rumor."

Questions to ask and points to ponder

It is interesting to see the students' amazement when the activity gets to the fifth step. They cannot believe how quickly the plague progresses even with each student contacting just one other student each time.

In a health curriculum, using an example like the plague in our activity is certainly a great way to demonstrate how quickly health concerns like the flu can spread throughout a population. It is also interesting to ask the students to ponder another point and to ask them if they notice what happens at the end of the activity.

At the end of the activity, the last number recorded is always smaller than whatever number preceded it. If there are 150 students on a team, after reaching 128 infected students, the next number to be infected is only 22. It is not that the plague is any less dangerous—it has simply run its course through this population. Eventually everyone that can be infected will be, and there is actually a decline in the number of people infected. Even a rumor will eventually run out of people that have not heard it. Unfortunately, a great deal of misinformation and hurt feelings happen first as the rumor moves quickly throughout the population.

There are many directions to go with this activity. It is eye-opening for the students. It is also a great staff activity to demonstrate how quickly rumors spread. No wonder the rumor mill is such an efficient operation!

Fire Brigade

This activity requires strategy, planning, and teamwork and is preparation for any future firemen in the classroom. This activity tests the students' creativity and helps them learn how to work together under pressure.

Materials needed

Provide one tablespoon per student and two cups per group. Large plastic cups work well. All of the cups should be the same size. Each group should have six to ten students.

Setting up the activity

All of the groups should start out with one cup about 3/4 full of water, and one empty cup. The task for the students is to pass the water from the full cup to the empty cup using the tablespoons. The first student dips out a spoonful of water and then passes it to the next student by pouring the water from her spoon to his spoon. The second student passes the water to the third student again by pouring the water from his spoon to the next spoon. The students may arrange themselves in any way they would like. Some will prefer a circle while others will form a straight line. They must move the water by pouring from one spoon into the next spoon. The water must go through all of the spoons in the group until the last spoon is poured into the cup to be filled.

Running the activity

Tell the students about how fire brigades years ago passed buckets of water from person to person to fight fires. Students will simulate the efforts of those early heroic fire brigades and pass water from one container to another. Depending on the amount of time available for this activity, set a time limit or let the students proceed until one group has emptied its first cup.

Then, carefully measure the second cup to see how much water the group was able to pass. To do this, pour each group's cup into a measuring cup, or you can dip a wooden ruler into the bottom of the cup. The activity sounds very wet, but actually the students spill very little, and there is only a 3/4 full cup for each group. Usually a few paper towels for each group will handle what spilling that might occur. Of course, if the activity is done outside, more water and bigger containers can be used. The size of the containers, and how much water to use, is up to each individual teacher.

Processing the activity

The first act of processing is declaring a winner—some sort of declaration of the best *Fire Brigade* in all the land. Be sure the students know that it is quite an honor to be treasured above all other honors.

Questions to ask and points to ponder

The pondering here can go several ways, but a good place to begin is by discussing the strategies the groups used and by discussing what worked and what did not. Always ask what the students would do differently if they had the chance. Some groups will form a circle, while others form a straight line. Some groups decide to have three people hold the six spoons and pour from their right hand to their left or vise versa before passing on to the next person. It is interesting that this method most often does not work very well. The fastest groups are usually the ones that use their favorite hands and use everyone in the group.

The winning groups find ways to make the distance shorter. One creative group held the spoons over each other so that any spill would just run down to the next spoon anyway. It is also interesting to watch the creative ways the groups will try to bend the rules. A great adaptation of this activity is to have everyone use the hand of least preference. "Lefties" must use their right hands and "righties" must use their left hands. With this adaptation, be prepared for a bit more spilled water.

There are many other points to ponder. A class may also discuss cooperation, problem solving, communication, trust, and the whole new respect they have for the fire brigades.

Tubular Dude

This activity gets the students into the tube as they see how fast they can move through a tire tube as a group.

Materials needed

This activity requires one bicycle tire tube and connectors for each student. A hula-hoop can be used instead of a tire tube. A tire tube makes the problem a little more challenging because of its flexibility.

It is a good idea to use connectors for this activity. Connectors are short ropes with loops at each end. Use cotton clothesline or some other rope and make each connector about a foot long. To do this, cut 3-foot pieces of rope and tie loops in each end so that the final product is about one foot long, including the loops. The idea of connectors is to allow students to hold hands without actually holding hands. If two students hold each end of a connector, they are connected as if they were holding hands, but they are about a foot apart. This allows for flexibility and eliminates all of the issues of holding hands. Some teachers have used things like bandannas or their blindfolds for connectors. Teachers may choose to use connectors any time an activity calls for the students to hold hands.

Setting up the activity

To set up this activity, get the students into a circle either holding hands or using the connectors to hold onto each other. Next, the teacher will break into the circle, put the tire tube or hula-hoop over the arm of one of the students, and reconnect the circle. Students are then challenged to pass the tire tube around the circle without breaking the circle until the tire tube gets back to where it started.

Running the activity

Explain to the students that they may not break the circle. If they do, they have to start over. Do not say anything about time on the first attempt to get the tire tube around the circle. After they move the tire tube around the circle once, challenge them to do it more quickly, and time their effort. Give them a few minutes to develop their strategy, and then they may try for speed. Groups may do the activity several times to achieve their fastest time.

It is also fun to get more than one tube going at the same time in opposite directions. This poses problems when the two tubes have to pass each other going in opposite directions. An added challenge is to have even more than two tubes going at once. Try sending two tubes going one way and two more going in the opposite direction. Another variation is to use a combination of tubes and hula-hoops. Be creative in imaging other varied challenges.

Processing the activity

This activity trains students to become accustomed to developing strategies together and then carrying out the strategies.

Questions to ask and points to ponder

The question to ask here is, "How does any group, yours in particular, develop strategies?" Talk about brainstorming and what that means. Then, talk about how one may make oneself heard in a group. Discuss how this group arrived at their decisions in this activity. A great question to ask is, "Does anyone have an idea that was not tried during the activity?" There usually are students that were unheard, so discuss why their ideas never emerged within the group. Did they not share it, or did the group not hear their suggestions? Then ask this question: how can people be heard in a group?

Read-Alouds

Read-alouds are not new, and they are a favorite student activity. A few favorites stories to read to students are listed below. The read-alouds shared here are stories that students have consistently enjoyed and that have meaning for middle level students' lives. After each read-aloud, discuss how the students might be able to apply what they interpreted from the story.

Materials needed

First, choose a story to read to the students. Two read-alouds are listed here, as are some great resources for additional stories.

Did I Ever Tell You How Lucky You Are?
By Dr. Seuss

Random House, Copyright 1973

Puppies for Sale
By Dan Clark

From Chicken Soup for the Soul

Dalmatian Press, Copyright 1999

Setting up the activity

Set up the classroom in a manner that is comfortable for reading to students. A room a little less formal than the traditional straight rows is always a nice change. Then, set the stage for the book to be read. For the story **Did I Ever Tell You How Lucky You Are?**, ask if students consider themselves to be lucky, and define "luck." Students at this age often feel the world is against them, and it is easy to get them to share why they feel they are unlucky. They might talk about other lucky kids that get to go to the mall, or go to parties, or wear more makeup, and so on. Once they are really feeling sorry for themselves, which is not difficult to achieve, read the story to them.

For the story **Puppies for Sale**, ask the students why people can be so cruel to each other. Every teacher has faced the problem of students picking on each other, especially at the middle level. Begin the class discussion by asking the students why people disrespect and pick on others in the first place, and who is most likely to be picked on. The students will probably share that anyone is pretty much fair game, but that anyone who is different or does not fit in will bear the brunt of the torment. After the discussion about disrespecting each other, read **Puppies for Sale** to them.

Processing the activity

Processing a well-chosen story is easy because it will relate to the students' real world. If they can relate to the story, not only will there be a good discussion, but it will also develop almost by itself.

Questions to ask and points to ponder

After reading the Dr. Seuss book **Did I Ever Tell You How Lucky You Are?**, the point is clear: No matter how bad a person's situation is, there is always someone out there that has it worse. So get over feeling sorry for yourself and get on with life! This is a great message for middle level students. After this lesson, when a student comes whining about something, the teacher should just hand them this book with a smile, and they usually get the message. Believe it or not, students have been known to borrow the book on their own to read again.

The story **Puppies for Sale** is very moving and really gets to students when read to a group. After reading this story, discuss the difference between sympathy and empathy. The lesson here is that people who are different need someone who really understands them. Certainly, no one needs ridicule. Someone who does not pick on someone, but ignores it or worse yet, laughs when it happens is nonetheless promoting it.

At one school, a group of students formed a club called the S.W.A.T. Team after reading and processing **Puppies for Sale**. S.W.A.T. stands for Students Working All Together, and the goal of the group was simply to help other students. For example, they created a circle of friends for students who might be picked on. Their goal was to always have five other students with that student making it clear that they did not approve of anyone picking on him or her. They invited students that did not have someone to sit with at lunch to sit with them at their lunch table. They provided mentors, tutors, and homework buddies for students that needed additional academic help. The incredible thing is that the students drove it all. All the students needed was a little push from **Puppies for Sale** and a little processing with a caring teacher.

The Team Puzzle

Students desperately want to fit in and are always trying to figure out their place. This activity will help students appreciate their individuality and uniqueness while demonstrating that they can and do fit in with the other students and the teachers.

Materials needed

This activity requires a team puzzle and a puzzle piece for each student and teacher on the team. The following demonstrates how to make the puzzle and pieces in setting up the activity.

Setting up the activity

Start by coming up with a team name and then move to building the puzzle. Use a roll of butcher paper three feet wide, and begin by pulling the paper over a table (the tables in the cafeteria work well for this) and block-lettering the team name across the paper. Make the largest letters possible, resulting in a large team banner. One option is to use a phrase with the team's name, like "The Manatees Rule!"

After the block letters are drawn, paint the letters with watercolors. Try using the team or school colors. When drawing and painting the letters, draw occasional connecting lines to give the banner a puzzle look. See the figure example below.

The next step is to make a copy of the banner. Pull the banner back over the table placing more butcher paper over the original and trace the banner. Do not color the traced copy because the copy will be cut. When making the copy, put a small number on the bottom of each piece; therefore, students will be able to tell top from bottom and which side is the front.

When the traced copy is complete, put the original away and cut out the traced copy. Cut up the copy on the lines and and around the letters. Throw away the letters. That way, when students put their pieces on the banner, the colored letters will show through. Now there is a banner and pieces to fit on the banner.

Running the activity

Now that the puzzle banner and the puzzle pieces are created, it is time for the activity. Give one piece of the puzzle to each student. Ask them to decorate their pieces of the puzzle in any way they would like, so long as it reflects them. For example, they might include their favorite CD cover, pictures of their families, friends, pets, vacation trips, their favorite sports team, and something that reflects their hobbies and interests like a picture of them downhill skiing, fishing, or singing. They may write, draw, or use pictures from home or magazines. Be sure to talk about what would be appropriate, and remind them to find the number on their piece so that they know which side to decorate and that they can tell top from bottom.

Let the students work on this over a period of several days so they can bring things from home, do the drawings, and find things that they want to put on their piece. Bring in magazines, and have masking tape or glue sticks for the students to use to attach things to their piece of the puzzle. When they have finished, go out in the hall where the banner has already been hung above the lockers or other suitable area. The students use duct or masking tape rings to attach their pieces to the banner.

Leave the banner up in the hallway or in one of the classrooms for quite a while, if not all year. Encourage students to add to their pieces of the puzzle throughout the year. Pictures taken during the year or examples of good class work can be added to the puzzle pieces. Always give the pieces back to the students to keep if they would like when the banner is taken off the wall.

Processing the activity

This is a great way for students to get to know their peers better. The activity actually shows students they can and do fit in. One student kept her piece of her team's puzzle until her graduation from high school. She shared with her teacher that she kept her piece of the puzzle and added to it each year. She put pictures from cheerleading, clubs, and other activities each year. After graduation, she put a picture of herself in her cap and gown and the wallet size copy of her diploma on her puzzle piece, had it framed, and still has it today as a great keepsake of her time in school.

Questions to ask and points to ponder

One of the points to make is that all students do have a place and can fit in with the other students. Just like the pieces, people come in all shapes, sizes, colors, and with a variety of interests. Students need to expect, respect, and appreciate diversity. Even with all of their differences, students can fit together quite well. Not everyone will be best friends, but everyone can respect differences and work together. Teachers want their students to appreciate what makes them unique and to know that they can fit in without giving up their uniqueness or dignity. A **Team Puzzle** is an excellent tool for teaching this important concept.

All About Me

Students relish talking about themselves. This activity puts students in the spotlight. It focuses on their thoughts and accomplishments.

Materials needed

Each student will need a *Me Sheet.* Choose one from page 104 or page 105.

Setting up the activity

Tell students that they will be constructing a sheet all about themselves. It is a good idea for the teacher to make one to use as a sample for the students. Tell students to bring in pictures, colored pencils, or other materials they would like to use.

Running the activity

Have students brainstorm each topic on the *Me Sheet.* Ask them to write their ideas on a piece of paper or to create a rough draft of the sheet. They should brainstorm these topics:

Goal in Life	Favorite Sport	Favorite Food	Something that makes you proud
Favorite Subject	Favorite Movie	Favorite Song	

Pass out a *Me Sheet* for each student to decorate. Encourage using a pen for writing the information; ink is easier to see.

Processing the activity

Students (and the teacher) learn a great deal of information about their classmates. Allow students the time to share the *Me Sheet* that they have created. Place the *Me Sheets* in an area for all to observe.

Questions to ask and points to ponder

Provided are two different *Me Sheets* from which teachers can select. Pick the one that is most interesting or ties into the class theme for the year.

Perhaps take this activity one step further and create a *Me Board*, *Me Box*, or *Me Mobile.* For the *Me Board,* provide students with a half sheet of poster board; they may create their own board from their experiences. For the *Me Box,* students need to cover a shoebox and create a box about themselves. Inside they may place something meaningful to them. For the *Me Mobile* they will need to use a hanger to create a mobile about their experiences. They decorate the board, box, or mobile with pictures, ribbons, magazine cutouts, and so on!

Me Sheet

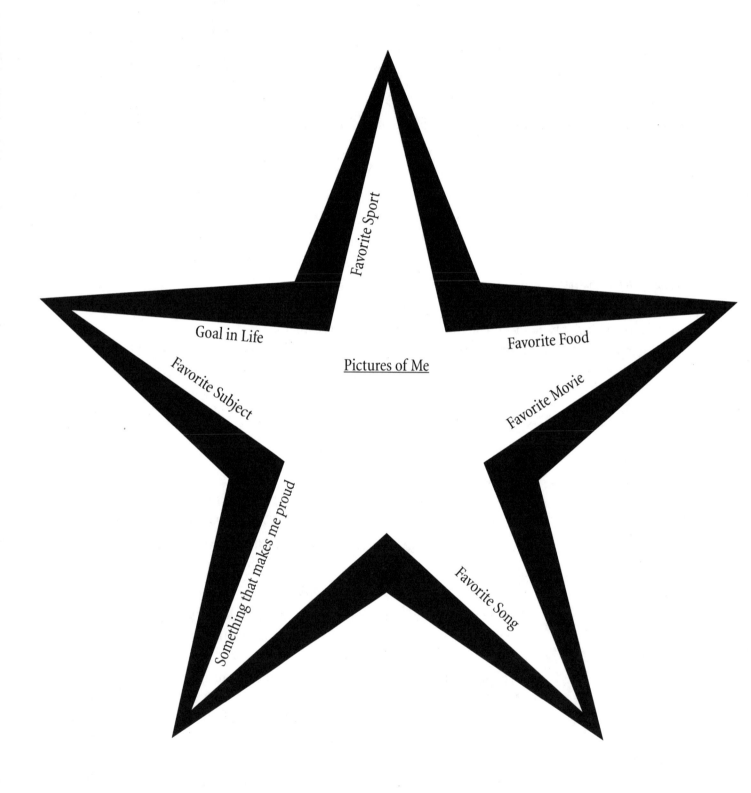

Favorite Sport

Goal in Life

Favorite Food

Pictures of Me

Favorite Subject

Favorite Movie

Something that makes me proud

Favorite Song

Me Sheet

Goal in Life	Favorite Movie
	Favorite Song

Favorite Food	Favorite Sport	Favorite Subject

Pictures of Me

Something that makes me proud

The Directions Game

The Directions Game is a motivating activity that will allow students to pick up cues in their environment and to recognize the importance of paying attention.

Materials needed

The Directions Game cards found on pages 108-111 and the Teacher Key on page 107.

Setting up the activity

Reproduce the cards on pages 108–111. Pass out a card to each student. If you have less than thirty students, some students will get two cards. The classroom door will need to be closed at the beginning of the game.

Running the activity

The Directions Game is based on a series of steps that students must follow. Students will receive a card that they will need to read in order to follow the directions indicated on the card.

Processing the activity

Students enjoy sharing what they think happened and what they could do to run the game more smoothly. *The Directions Game* is enjoyable and practical. Please take the time to try this strategy in class; teachers are truly amazed at the discussion following the activity. After teachers have students' attention with a motivating activity, it is easy to talk about the concept of following directions. Stress the importance of picking up on subtle cues such as reading the directions first or distinguishing between standing and marching.

Questions to ask and points to ponder

Teachers are constantly trying to get students to listen up and follow directions. *The Directions Game* is a fun and motivating technique to emphasize following directions. Students frequently request to play the game. They like to time themselves and to see if they are able to improve their score. Students like to challenge other classes to beat their time and enjoy switching cards and playing again.

Even though teachers have a key as the students are playing the game, the students should not be stopped during the process. Allow students to finish what they started and to see if they can determine what they need to correct if any mistakes are made. At the end of the game, all players should have completed the task indicated on their card. If they have not, they are well aware that the class did not follow directions clearly.

Directions Game

This is a key for the teacher to use while following along.

Directions

1. You are going to start this game! Say, "Ready, set, go!" when you are ready.

2. After someone says, "Ready, set, go!" stand up and clap four times.

3. When someone claps four times, stand up and honk like a goose.

4. After someone honks like a goose, sharpen your pencil.

5. After someone in the room sharpens a pencil, stand up and put one hand in the air for eight seconds.

6. When someone puts one hand in the air, write your first name on the board.

7. After someone writes his or her name on the board, stomp your foot four times.

8. Once someone stomps his or her foot four times, write the numbers 1-5 on the board.

9. After someone writes the numbers 1-5 on the board, stand up and spin around two times.

10. When someone spins around two times, say, "Good Job!"

11. After someone says, "Good Job!" erase the person's name from the board.

12. After someone erases the name from the board, erase the numbers 1-5.

13. When someone erases the numbers 1-5 from the board, say the alphabet aloud.

14. Once someone says the alphabet aloud, say the time aloud.

15. After someone says the time aloud, say today's date aloud.

16. After someone says the date aloud say, "Shh! QUIET!"

17. When someone says, "Shh! QUIET!" say, "Help, I want out of here!"

18. After someone says, "Help, I want out of here!" yell out the name of a TV show.

19. After someone yells out a TV show, turn off half of the lights.

20. After someone turns off half of the lights, write "Smile" on the board.

21. When someone writes "Smile" on the board, open the door.

22. When someone opens the door, snap your fingers five times.

23. When someone snaps his or her fingers five times, march in place for seven seconds.

24. After someone marches in place for seven seconds, turn all the lights on.

25. Once someone turns the lights on, close the door.

26. After someone closes the door, stand up and say aloud your favorite color.

27. After someone says a color aloud, say "Stop it!"

28. After someone says, "Stop it!" erase the word "Smile" from the board.

29. After someone erases the word "Smile" from the board, go stand by the teacher's desk.

30. When someone stands by the teacher's desk, write "The End" on the board.

You are going to start this game! Say, "Ready, set, go!" when you are ready.

After someone says, "Ready, set, go!" stand up and clap four times.

When someone claps four times, stand up and honk like a goose.

After someone honks like a goose, sharpen your pencil.

After someone in the room sharpens a pencil, stand up and put one hand in the air for eight seconds.

When someone puts one hand in the air, write your first name on the board.

After someone writes his or her name on the board, stomp your foot four times.

Once someone stomps his or her foot four times, write the numbers 1–5 on the board.

After someone writes the numbers 1-5 on the board, stand up and spin around two times.

When someone spins around two times, say, "Good Job!"

After someone says, "Good Job!" erase the person's name from the board.

After someone erases the name from the board, erase the numbers 1-5.

When someone erases the numbers 1-5 from the board, say the alphabet aloud.

Once someone says the alphabet aloud, say the time aloud.

After someone says the time aloud, say today's date aloud.

After someone says the date aloud say, "Shh! QUIET!"

When someone says, "Shh! QUIET!" say, "Help, I want out of here!"

After someone says, "Help, I want out of here!" yell out the name of a TV show.

After someone yells out a TV show, turn off half of the lights.

After someone turns off half of the lights, write "Smile" on the board.

When someone writes "Smile" on the board, open the door.

When someone opens the door, snap your fingers five times.

When someone snaps his or her fingers five times, march in place for seven seconds.

After someone marches in place for seven seconds, turn all the lights on.

Once someone turns the lights on, close the door.

After someone closes the door, stand up and say aloud your favorite color.

After someone says a color aloud, say "Stop it!"

After someone says, "Stop it!" erase the word "Smile" from the board.

After someone erases the word "Smile" from the board, go stand by the teacher's desk.

When someone stands by the teacher's desk, write "The End" on the board.

Exciting Group Activities for Team Building

Big Foot

This is a favorite activity because the students are astounded by what they can do. This activity takes getting one foot up on someone to a whole new level!

Materials needed

There are no materials needed for this activity.

Setting up the activity

Split the class into two groups. Tell the groups that they are an engineering and construction company and that they build towers.

Running the activity

This activity can be run in several ways. One way is explained here, but it can be easily adapted to any classroom's circumstances. The challenge here is to see which company can build their tower the closest to the exact specifications given. Consider adding a time constraint as well, such as five minutes to complete the tower.

The towers must be made with student feet. Shoes must stay on, and students simply put one foot on top of another, toe-to-heel, until they have stacked their feet exactly $51\frac{3}{4}$ inches tall. The fun part is watching them use different combinations of feet to get as close to exactly $51\frac{3}{4}$ inches as they can. Cut several pieces of string to the target height so that the groups can use the string as a measuring tool. The challenge is to get the foot tower as close to the exact height as possible.

Stacking student feet to heights less than 5 feet usually does not require any lifting. It is possible to ask groups to build taller towers; however, the students will need instruction in spotting and lifting techniques. Groups have been known to stack their feet up to the basketball rims in the gym or the goal posts outside. Additionally, if the towers are tall, provide mats, while reminding them about spotting and lifting. For those teachers who are not familiar with spotting and lifting techniques, keep the height under 5 feet and attempt a specific measurement and speed. Give the groups a few minutes to plan their strategies before beginning the activity.

The first group to the mark wins. If selecting a particular height, the easiest way to measure it is to give each group a piece of string or rope cut to the height. The group can use the string to measure as they go. Or, put a mark on the wall with tape, and the students can put their feet against the wall, stacking them until they reach the mark. Of course, the students could just put their feet heel-to-toe on the floor, but that would not be as challenging or as entertaining!

Processing the activity

This activity requires planning and strategy. The students have to work together considering shoe size, leg length, and so on. Of course, the students with the big feet become very popular at this time.

Questions to ask and points to ponder

This is a great trust-building and problem-solving activity. In this activity the "smart" students are not always the stars, and the students learn to appreciate the different talents of their classmates. Ask the students what the challenges were as they tried to stack their feet to match a specific height.

One of the challenges is communication. "Move to the left" often gets the response, "Who's left?" or "No, your other left!" as they try to work together. Cooperative learning depends on the students being able to focus on a task and not on personalities. In this activity, students really become focused on the feet, and every person in the group is essential as the groups try different combinations of feet to achieve the exact height.

Land Mine Clearing

With a great deal of international pressure, countries are being encouraged to forgo the use of land mines. Unfortunately, in the areas of the world where land mines have been used over the years, there are still mines in the fields that pose a threat to those living there. For this exercise, students are going to become a part of a team of specialists that will find and dispose of mines—talk about a challenging job!

Materials needed

First, build a minefield in the classroom, the cafeteria, an outside court, or paved parking lot. To build a minefield, make a 10 x 10 matrix on the floor with masking tape like the one shown below. Make each of the lines at least a foot apart. If there is enough room, make them 18 to 24 inches apart.

Draw a matrix on a sheet of paper like the one shown below. This will be the teacher's map of the minefield. Put Xs on the sheet to show where the mines are going to be located. Do not put the Xs on the floor—just the lines forming the squares. Change the location of the mines each time the class embarks on this activity. The students do not get to see the map of the minefield. The map is for the teacher's eyes only.

Sample matrix

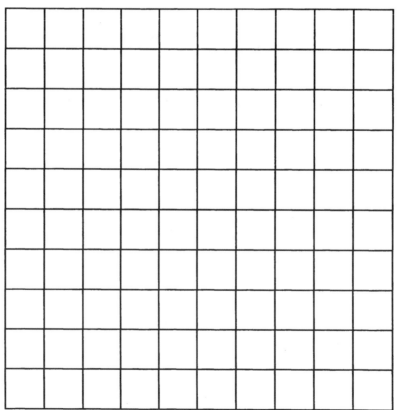

Setting up the activity

Show the students the minefield and tell them about the mines that remain in some countries threatening the people who live there. Remind them of children who are unaware as they innocently play in the minefields. Explain that their class is a specialized unit of mine removers that travels the world taking out mines. Their job is to make the world a safer place. In order to be ready on a moment's notice, the team must constantly train to work on their skills. This activity simulates one of many rigorous training drills.

Running the activity

Divide the students into two or more teams. Tell them they have to start on one side and get their team across the minefield. They cannot see where the mines are, but the teacher has a map showing where each mine is located. Each team must step into the minefield and follow each other across. If a team steps on a mine, that team must start over. After each step, the teacher will tell the team if their leader has stepped on a mine. Each time a team starts over, a different team member has to take the lead.

As a team moves across the minefield, the members must follow the leader, stepping only where the leader has stepped. The leader may move one step at a time in any direction. The team members will form a "caterpillar" as they follow the leader one step at a time. Since a different student must take the lead each time the team starts over, they have to work together to cross the minefield.

Whenever a team hits a mine, which happens often, they wait outside the minefield while another team takes their turn. While teams wait, they can decide what path they are going to try next and who will lead the group. The teams need to not only remember where the mines are that they have hit but also where the mines are that the other teams have hit so they do not hit those, either. The first team across the minefield is the winner.

Processing the activity

Each group will get many opportunities to start over, develop strategies, and decide on the new leaders while they work together to get across the minefields. The students like strategy games and really get into this activity.

Questions to ask and points to ponder

Consensus is not always easy to reach, and the teams have to reach consensus for each step. One point to ponder is how groups made their decisions each time they would meet after stepping on a mine. Try to get the class to discuss the theories that the teams developed, such as the theory that mines are never located behind each other. This is also a great opportunity to talk about the difference between inductive and deductive reasoning.

Have A Seat!

For anyone who has ever been in a room where there are more people than there are seats, this will be a welcome activity. In this activity, the students will demonstrate how to become the chairs themselves and will learn to sit without seats.

Materials needed

No materials are needed for this activity.

Setting up the activity

For this activity, take the students outside or to an open area like the cafeteria. Tell them that they are going to create a way to sit down without chairs. To demonstrate, ask one student to sit on a chair and have another student sit on that student's knees. Make sure the student sits out on the knees and not on the other student's lap. The student should be as far out on the other student's knees as possible. Then ask another student to sit on the second student's knees in the same way, and then another, and another until there are four or five students sitting on each other's knees to demonstrate the procedure. During the activity, remove the chair.

Running the activity

Tell the students that the challenge for the group is to have the entire class sitting on each other's knees. The challenge here is to achieve this without the use of any chairs. Put the students into a circle, and then ask them to turn to their left so that each person in the circle can put his or her hands on the shoulders of the student in front of him. Then they are to sit as a group on each other's knees. They will "overlap" (every pun intended). The group should squat as they would when they go to sit in a chair, except that they are going to sit on the knees of the person behind them. They have achieved their goal when every student is "seated" in the circle.

Needless to say, the group will not be successful in the first few attempts; when they are successful, students are impressed by their accomplishment. Some groups have asked to do the activity again so a picture could be taken of them to show unbelieving friends and family.

Processing the activity

This is a challenge that initially does not sound possible. Students like to achieve the seemingly impossible.

Questions to ask and points to ponder

The first question to ask the students is "What did you think about doing this activity?" They will talk about how they did not think it was possible at first. Talk about how ordinary people can do extraordinary things when they trust and support each other and work together.

The next point to ponder is that there is a high element of trust in this activity. This is a great activity that demonstrates what the students can do when they learn they can lean on each other for support. *Lean On Me*—what a great message!

Students who cannot participate in this activity due to knee or leg injuries or handicaps can be included by helping their classmates circle up before the activity, by encouraging others, and by offering an onlooker's perspective in the follow-up discussion.

Fast Ball

This activity is an adaptation of the *Juggling It All* activity. It is a challenging activity to get students working together to solve a problem. *Fast Ball* is fun and motivating while being a difficult challenge for the students. Students will have a great time while improving their problem-solving skills, as well.

Materials needed

Provide students with one of the balls from the juggling activity.

Setting up the activity

This activity is set up just like the juggling activity. Put the students into a circle. This activity works well for groups up to about forty but becomes difficult with groups larger than that. Conduct **Fast Ball** in an open area large enough for the group to get into a circle and toss the ball to each other.

Running the activity

This activity starts just like the juggle activity. Pick a student, "Walt," to start the activity. Give Walt the ball and have him call out a student's name and toss him or her the ball. Then have that student pick someone else, call her name and toss her the ball. Do the same for the third student and then review the "rules." Remind them about appropriate throws and calling the name first. Also remind students about keeping their hands in front of them if they have not caught the ball and keeping their hands behind them after they have caught the ball. After everyone in the circle has touched the ball one time, the last person will call out Walt's name and toss the ball back to Walt.

The pattern will be random as students toss the ball. When everyone has caught and tossed the ball, tell the students that all they have to remember is the person who caught their ball. After everyone has caught the ball once and the ball has made it back to Walt, have the students repeat sending the ball around the circle; however, this time they must call the name, and throw the ball to the same person as last time. At this point, students must always throw to that same person. Practice at least once.

During the second practice, without telling the students, time how long it takes the ball to get around the circle, starting and ending with Walt. Since students have not been told to toss the ball around quickly, it usually takes a minute or so to get the ball from start to finish. For purposes of this demonstration, assume it took 90 seconds for the ball to get around the circle.

This is where the fun starts! Tell the group that the federal government has done tests and has determined that a group of this size should be able to get the ball around in half the time that it took them the first time. The challenge is that this group should be able to get the ball around the circle in 45 seconds. The ball must touch each person in the same order. Since students practiced the order, do not ask them to call out each name as they go for speed. It usually is not very difficult for them to cut the time in half.

As students work to get the ball around more and more quickly, they come up with all sorts of ideas. Usually the first thing they do is move the circle in, and then they change the order of the circle so that each person is standing next to the person they need to throw the ball to. Students then simply hand the ball off to the person next to them. Some groups form two straight lines, put their hands together, and pass the ball between them. One group moved the ball so fast we almost could not time them. They went to the cafeteria and put one end of one of the tables down to form a ramp. They put their fingers down in the correct order, and let the ball roll over their fingers. Each group uses different strategies, but every group has been able to get the ball around, touching each person in the correct order, in less than 10 seconds!

Just how fast a group may get the ball around will also depend on how much time is available for them to work. Regardless of how quickly they finally get the ball around to everyone, they will have a great time while working hard. Teachers will be amazed by the students' creativity.

Processing the activity

Teamwork, cooperation, sharing, listening, openness to new ideas, determination, and thinking out of the box are just a few of the things students can discuss after this activity.

Questions to ask and points to ponder

Of course, one of the first questions to ask is, "What did it take to get the ball around the circle in the fastest time?" They will discuss rearranging the circle and who initially had the different ideas. Point out how many different ideas it took to get to the final result. Some of the suggestions did not work well, but often led to others that did. Another point to ponder is how hard students were willing to work, even when ideas did not work on the first try. Talk to students about applying this energy to both schoolwork and homework.

The Gator Swamp

This activity works well with a large group. *The Gator Swamp* has several powerful messages for students and staff; it demonstrates communication skills and develops trust. People who have ever had to deal with rumors, locker chat, or "He said"/ "She said" situations are going to love this activity!

Materials needed

Provide 10–15 hula hoops (any size), self-stick notes or other small pieces of paper, and possibly some masking tape for marking off an area for taping down the small pieces of paper. Blindfolds are also needed for each student. Try using cut up sheets for the blindfolds; be sure to wash them after each use.

Setting up the activity

This activity requires a large open area, such as the cafeteria or the gymnasium. Mark off a rectangular area with masking tape. The volleyball area marked off in most gyms is ideal for this activity. In the cafeteria, make the rectangle as large as possible, staying about 10 feet in from the walls. Randomly toss the hula-hoops into the marked rectangular area.

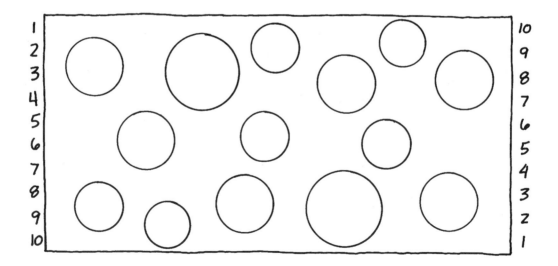

Sort the students into groups of five or six. If there are 10 groups, write the numbers 1–10 on the pieces of paper or self-stick notes. Put one number on each piece of paper, and make two sets of numbered notes. Place the numbers on the floor as evenly spaced as possible across one side of the area. Then put the second set on the floor on the opposite side of the area in the reverse order, as illustrated here.

Running the activity

Before going to the cafeteria, assign each student a number by having the students count off one through the total number of groups. Pick one of the numbered sides to start the activity, take all of the students to the cafeteria, and have the students then stand behind their number. The ones stand behind the #1, the twos stand behind the #2, and so on. Everybody with the same number becomes a team, and they should stand in a line behind their number.

Tell the students that the area they see before them represents a gator swamp. Each one of the hula-hoops represents a gator hole. Their task is to get their team across the gator swamp without touching or stepping in one of the gator holes. What happens when someone steps in a gator hole? Chomp, chomp—and that person will have to go back and start again. Point out the numbers on the other side, and tell the students they have to go to their number on the other side. Since the numbers are in reverse order, they will be crisscrossing the swamp to get to their destination.

Unfortunately, swamps are often very foggy, and it is difficult to see. To simulate that, any person going across must be blindfolded, making the game more interesting and fun. They only have to wear the blindfold when they are in the swamp. When they have crossed, they may take their blindfolds off. Each team may send only one person at a time across the swamp. When one person is completely across, then another team member may begin to cross the swamp.

The team will send one member across the swamp and can position the other members anywhere they would like, except inside the swamp, to help their teammate get across. Most teams will position members along the sides and at their number on the opposite side so that they can yell instructions to their teammate to help get him or her to their number on the opposite side. When one team member gets across, another one will go to the starting side, put his blindfold on, and begin to cross the swamp. The activity continues until every student crosses the swamp.

After presenting the instructions to the teams, give students three to five minutes to brainstorm about how they are going to get each other across the swamp. Many teams will walk into the swamp to map out their best route. They will position each other around the swamp and decide how to get instructions to whoever is in the swamp. Tell the students that one of the teachers has gator-proof shoes and will be in the swamp. If a student touches one of the gator holes, the teacher will tap him on the shoulder and send him back to start over.

What students do not know is that once the activity begins, the teacher is going to start kicking the hula-hoops all over the place. Try to kick them right in front of students! The teams really start yelling now to let their person know that the hoops are being kicked around. Make it challenging for the teams to get across, and it can be entertaining for the facilitator. Needless to say, the activity will get crazy with students running all over the place and with all of the teams trying to yell instructions to their teammates.

Processing the activity

This is a high-energy activity, and one that the students really like to talk about! Start by saying, "You were pretty confident when we started. Some of you had your route already planned, and you thought that it was not going to be as difficult as it turned out to be."

Questions to ask and points to ponder

The first question to ask is, "What made crossing the gator swamp more difficult than you first thought it was going to be?" Remind the students that no one said that the hoops would not be moved and that their task was to come up with the best strategy to get their team across the swamp.

Try asking the students, "Do you ever come to school thinking things are going to go one way and then things change without warning?" They might share pop quiz experiences, relationship break-ups, forgetting assignments, and many other surprise

experiences. The next question is, "How do you deal with situations that do not go as you expect?" Students may then discuss who they can go to for help when things appear to be getting out of hand.

The question to begin pondering point two is, "In addition to the moving hoops, what else made the activity difficult?" Here the discussion turns to how loud it was and how difficult it was to hear his or her teammates. Ask, "What was everybody yelling to their teammates?" Ask the students, "Do you ever get mixed messages and have two or more people telling you different things? How do you decide who to listen to?" People often hear two or three different opinions; each one may sound very good, and it is sometimes difficult to know who to listen to. Those students who listen to the right people will get through the swamps with much fewer problems. Those students who listen to the rumor mill or to the wrong person will get the wrong information. With the wrong information, people make the wrong decisions, which can lead to all kinds of trouble.

The students really take off with this discussion when they are encouraged to share times when they listened to the wrong person. Then, ask whom they can go to when faced with a decision to make. The students will list their friends as ones they can trust, but they will also list their teachers, parents, religious leaders, and so on. Learning to be careful about whom one listens to is a valuable lesson. This is one activity where the students really get into the processing of the activity.

Be A Brain

Teachers all want their students to become the best students they can be. To do this, it is very helpful if the students understand how the brain works and how they can take advantage of the various learning situations they will encounter in school. In this activity, the students will actually get to go inside a brain and learn a little about how it works.

Materials needed

The teacher will need a list of left-brain and right-brain descriptors. A great list can be found in the book **Learning to Learn**, by Gloria Frender, published by Incentive Publications.

Setting up the activity

Take the students to the football or soccer field for this one. Then, ask the students to get into a line in front of the teacher as if they were in a line at the movie theatre. Tell the students that the teacher will call several descriptors for them to ponder. Then, ask them to take a step to the left or right for each descriptor. As the activity progresses, they will continue to move left or right and will be more and more spread out.

Running the activity

Read descriptors like these from the book **Learning to Learn**.

1. I learn best by seeing and hearing.

2. I learn best by touching or doing.

3. I am usually aware of time.

4. I sometimes rely on my intuition when making decisions.

5. I notice and remember details.

With each descriptor, ask the students to move left or right. For example, read number one above for all of the students to hear. Then say, "If this sounds like you, take a giant step to your left. If this does not sound like you, take a giant step to your right."

For number two above, say "If this sounds like you, take a giant step to your right. If this does not sound like you, take a giant step to your left." Of course, with each one, the students will move to their left or to their right. It is interesting to watch the line split after each descriptor.

Throw in a few descriptors that are just for fun. Most of these do not have anything to do with left-brain or right-brain dominance:

1. *Take a small step forward. If you stepped with your left foot, move to your left, if you stepped with your right foot, step to your right.*

2. *Clasp your hands together. If your right thumb is on top, move to your right. If your left thumb is on top, move to your left. If they are beside each other, do not move.*

3. *Turn around and face the other side of the field. Now, continue turning in the same direction until you are facing us again. If you turned counterclockwise, take a step to your left. If you turned clockwise, take a step to your right.*

4. *Give us your best wink. If you winked with your left eye, step to your left. If you winked with your right eye, take a step to your right. If you used both eyes and are biwinkle, stay where you are.*

5. *Pretend there is a giant easel behind you. Put your hand in the air, and draw the outline of a horse. If your horse faces to the left, take a step to your left. If your horse faces to the right, take a step to the right.*

Teachers can come up with additional creative descriptors to go with the real ones. Using just a few of these will not disrupt the left-brain or right-brain results and will add even more fun to the activity.

Continue this process until the students are getting really spread out. Then, have the students walk straight toward the teacher from wherever they are at the end of the descriptors. Since they are very spread out, when they walk toward the teacher they begin to form a semicircle, which the teacher should encourage and help them form.

Processing the activity

Watch the students as they move through this activity. No one will move only left or right, but teachers can often predict which way some students are going to move most of the time. It is important to point out to students that they all took some steps in both directions.

Questions to ask and points to ponder

After the students are in the semicircle in front of the teacher, tell them that they have formed the Human Brain. Walk into the left part of the brain, and ask questions like, "How do you organize the money in your wallet or purse?"

While walking around inside the brain, continue to ask questions. Here are some questions that demonstrate to students how they all think differently.

1. How does your locker look?

2. How does your bedroom at home look?

3. Do you know before you wake up what you are going to wear on a particular day?

4. How do you organize your clothes in your closet?

5. What is your favorite kind of class?

Talk about the things that make us all different. It is important that the teacher shares as well.

For the grand finale, ask the students to cross their arms in front of them. Do not ask them to move, just to cross their arms. Tell them that just like all of the other things talked about, some of them have placed their right arm over their left, while others have their left arm over their right. Then, ask them to cross their arms the "wrong way." Crossing their arms the wrong way is often very difficult for students. Tell them to hold their arms crossed in the wrong way until they are told they can uncross their arms.

Now cross your own arms and state that some students learn this way; then cross your arms the other way, while stating that some students learn this way. Cross arms back the other way, and tell students that some of their classes are taught this way; then cross arms the other way, and tell them that some of their classes will be taught this way.

Students will not always feel comfortable in their classes. Remind students that being uncomfortable should not be mistaken for being stupid. Just because a student learns one way, and a class is sometimes taught another way, does not make a student stupid or the teacher a bad teacher.

Now, ask the students to shake out their arms. Then, immediately ask them to cross their arms the "wrong way" again. It will still be uncomfortable, but they will be able to do a little better, and it will not be as uncomfortable as before. The point to ponder with students is that while they may not be comfortable in all of their classes all of the time, they should not think that they cannot be successful in that class.

Follow up this activity with strategies to help the students successfully learn in different classroom situations. This is one of the more powerful activities to do with students; they will remember which side of the brain they tend to use more often.

Java Move

Java Move is similar to speed ball, but uses a coffee can instead of a ball. Students need to work together to solve a problem. Students will have a good time finding a solution and will try to master their skill each time they play.

Materials needed

One empty coffee can (any size will work) will be needed.

Setting up the activity

Begin *Java Move* by putting the class into a circle. *Java Move* works well with groups smaller than forty students; if there are more students, divide them into two groups, and get an additional coffee can.

An open area is required for this activity. Grab the coffee can, move to an open area, and have students get into a big circle.

Running the activity

Select a student to begin the activity. Simply tell the students that they are going to pass the coffee can around without dropping it. The starter will start passing the can around the circle. When the can makes it back to her, this part of the activity will stop. Have the students pass the can around once. After they understand the process have them do the task again. This time, the teacher should time the students without the students knowing that they are being timed. After the can reaches the starter, tell them how long it took. They will immediately want to time themselves again to improve their score.

Once students have timed themselves and feel good about the time they have achieved, move on to the next step of *Java Move*. Tell them that there is a problem. Everyone's hands have just been covered with sticky tar, and they cannot touch the coffee can or it will stick in the tar. So, now students need to pass the can around the circle without using their hands. Do not time the activity; passing the can is the most important assignment at this point. This is a good point to select another student to begin the activity. Students often need to help one another in passing the can. Teachers will be amazed at how creative students will be with this activity.

Processing the activity

There are many points to emphasize when processing **Java Move**. The students will be able to identify and discuss many of the related topics. They realize that teamwork and cooperation are necessary to pass the can. Other issues to discuss are sharing, listening, determination, and new ideas for speed.

Questions to ask and points to ponder

Discussing with the students why some ideas worked and some ideas did not is a great motivator. This is easy to relate to real world situations. When teachers choose to share some of their experiences, the students are eager to listen, and they are willing to share as well. Students like to elaborate on how to move the can faster though the circle. They are often quite creative during this discussion.

Students often share that it was frustrating not being able to use their hands. This opens up a variety of topics for discussion, from diversity to homework. Some attempts are frustrating but if a new approach is attempted, often a solution is found that is better than the original plan. Students begin to discover that many minds are better that just one.

One time a discussion about special needs students came out of this activity. The discussion began with how difficult it was not to be able to use one's hands. Students related that to a handicapped child in the building and how frustrating it must be for him at times. The kids realized that the things they take for granted are not available to all people.

Scavenger Hunt

The **Scavenger Hunt** allows students to discover techniques to encourage group collaboration and to create group identity.

Materials needed

Each student will need a list of items to collect for the **Scavenger Hunt**. Teachers may make up their own list or use the sample list in this activity.

Setting up the activity

Make sure the hall or wing outside the classroom is free from activity the day of a scavenger hunt. Divide students into groups of three for this activity.

Running the activity

Send students on a hunt throughout the school, hall, or room. Give each team a list of items to find and a time limit. The suggested time limit for the **Scavenger Hunt** is fifteen minutes. A sample hunt is listed on the following page.

Processing the activity

A scavenger hunt is a great way to emphasize cooperation. Discuss with students the different strategies their groups used to find the various items.

Questions to ask and points to ponder

When the students are finished with the scavenger hunt, it is a good idea to discuss strategy. Some questions to ask might include the following: "How did you locate items? What did you do in your group? What worked well? What did not work well?"

After students share their experiences, emphasize the importance of teams and working together. Teachers may share examples from their own lives. Students are fascinated to learn that their teachers work together outside of the classroom.

Remember to make sure students are able to obtain the items on the list. Students must be able to achieve the goal set forth.

Scavenger Hunt

You will have fifteen minutes to gather the items listed below.

You may not leave the academic wing or interrupt any classes.

Remember to ask permission if you are using an item that belongs to someone else. Return the item when you are finished.

Good luck!

_____ *A pencil*

_____ *A notebook*

_____ *A plastic bag*

_____ *Two pennies*

_____ *One shoelace*

_____ *A magnet*

_____ *One square of toilet paper*

_____ *A photograph*

_____ *A brush*

_____ *A rubber band*

_____ *A test or quiz*

_____ *A paper clip*

Love Those Lists

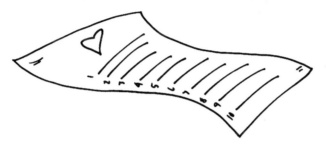

This activity encourages brainstorming and working together to generate ideas and solve problems. Students are given time to work together to be as creative as possible. *Love Those Lists* is a great way to stimulate creative thinking.

Materials needed

Provide something for each group of students on which to record their lists. Mini-marker boards, mini-chalkboards, or paper will work. If you are using marker boards, provide a dry erase marker and an eraser (a tissue works well) for each group. If using a chalkboard, make sure there is enough chalk and an eraser for each group.

First, cut 3" x 3" squares in four different colors. Label numbers one through four on the cards. It is a good idea to make each number a different color. For example, write a number "1" on each blue card, a number "2" on each orange card, and so on.

Setting up the activity

Determine what categories are to be used for the activity. Put students into groups of three or four. A group recorder should be selected for each team. There are some ground rules to establish with students prior to using groups. Some ideas are:
1. Do not criticize ideas.
2. Everyone should contribute.
3. Brainstorm everything.
4. All ideas are good.
5. Build on the ideas of others.

Running the activity

Each group will list as many ideas as possible for a given topic. Tell them the topic, and they will list the ideas. For example, ask the students to list as many things as they can think of that are blue.

Listed below are some topic ideas.
    Types of quadrilaterals
    Prepositions
    Countries and capitals
    Greek gods and goddesses
    Parts of a cell
    Insects

Tell the students they have time to brainstorm and list everything they can for each topic selected. Determine a time limit that works well for the topic; approximately eight minutes is a good brainstorming session. Students will share ideas, and the recorder will write down the information on the marker board or paper.

When time is up for a specific topic, have students put the caps on the dry erase markers or put their pencils down. Ask a team to share its list with the class. Each team's name will be written on the board. After the team reads an item, have students raise their hand if they have that item. From the hands raised after each item is read aloud, determine each team's score. Use the guidelines below:

If a member of each team raises his or her hand, that means every team has arrived at the same answer; therefore, no team "wins" that round, and no points are given for that response.

If four teams have the response, a 1-point card is given to each team.

If three teams share the response, a 2-point card is given to each team.

If two teams share the response, a 3-point card is given to each team.

If only one team has the answer, a 4-point card is given to that team.

Processing the activity

Students enjoy working in groups to figure out all possible answers. They realize that sometimes they overlook the obvious, and this realization generates a good discussion. Students also realize that being creative is a positive experience, and they try to be innovative with this activity.

Questions to ask and points to ponder

Teachers may decide to use counters to keep track of the score or numbers on the board; or vary the game and have a different recorder each time during the process. Chart paper may also be used for recording information.

This activity is helpful to use when introducing the importance of brainstorming and working together. Students often see that the group knows more than one person alone. **Love Those Lists** helps students learn to be cooperative contributors in their groups.

Just For Fun

The Leaning Tower of Pizza

Teachers know that many middle school students think with their stomachs. Mention food, and a teacher has students' undivided attention. Come to think of it, mention food, and often achieve undivided adult attention as well!

Materials needed

The students are going to be building towers, and a variety of materials may be used. Choose from some of the materials listed, or use other materials. Jellybeans and toothpicks, marshmallows and toothpicks, straws, newspaper with a little tape, a deck of cards, a pack of 3 x 5 cards, or any combination of these and other materials will work.

Setting up the activity

Tell the students that they have been hired to build the greatest tower of all time. An alternative is to ask them to go for the tallest tower or the most creative or to leave it up to each group to decide what kind of tower they want to build. Make the activity more interesting and challenging by telling the students that they are not allowed to talk while building the tower.

Running the activity

First, put the students into groups. Once the criteria for the towers is decided, tell the students what materials they will use. Favorite materials are marshmallows and straws. Then, set a time limit for them to accomplish the task.

When the groups are finished, judge the towers, and enjoy the leftovers. The nice thing about using jellybeans and marshmallows is that students can eat any of the unused building materials as well.

Processing the activity

It is hard to lose when you are working with sweets! There is also a lot of strategy that goes into the design of the towers and into the problem solving when they begin to fold. This is a hands-on activity that the students will really enjoy.

Questions to ask and points to ponder

Begin by getting the students to discuss the various strategies that they used to build their towers. Some will use triangles while others will use rectangles. Some will build a large base, and some will go for tall and skinny. Some of the towers will fall while others will stand.

If the students completed this activity nonverbally, discuss how they communicated with each other. How were they able to get others to understand what they wanted them to do, and how did they exchange ideas?

This activity allows for students to eat the materials and have a great discussion with their teacher.

A Pat on the Back

Everyone needs and deserves a little pat on the back occasionally. The only problem is that there is not always someone there to give that pat on the back when it is needed. The *Pat On The Back* activity will help students remember their positive qualities. This is a great activity for staff as well!

Materials needed

Provide heavy construction paper, writing pens, and straight pins or masking tape for each student. Try using file folders cut in half to create a stiff surface for writing.

Setting up the activity

The first thing to do is to ask the students to trace their hands on their piece of paper. Then, students work in pairs to put their traced hands on their backs so that the traced hand faces out. If using masking tape, give each student two pieces of tape, long enough to go over their own shoulders. Straight pins work well, but carefully consider the inherent risks with pins. When all the students have their hands secured to their backs, begin the activity.

Running the activity

Tell the students that they are to move around the room and write on every other student's "hand." With a large class, tell the students to write on at least fifteen other hands. They should write something positive about each person. It must be specific about that person; it is beneficial if the teacher shares several examples for the students. Since the hands are on their backs, students cannot see what others are writing on them.

Also tell the students not to sign what they write—messages should be anonymous. Try to have some music playing while the students are moving around the room and writing on each other's backs. It is fun to watch the human chains develop as groups begin to write on each other's "hands." There will often be ten or more students in a line, slightly bent over, as they write. When all the students have written on all the hands, stop the music, and have the students move to their seats.

When the students get to their seats, ask them to remove their hands from their backs and read what everyone has written about them. It is fun to watch them read what everyone has written. Those who have ever watched students when yearbooks come out will not be surprised by how eager they are to read what the other students have written.

Processing the activity

Everyone experiences times when things are not going their way and they get down on themselves. It is important to remember our strengths, and it is very meaningful to have a way for our peers to point out those strengths. One teacher kept her *Pat on the Back* for many years and still uses it when she needs some encouragement.

Questions to ask and points to ponder

Tell the students that they should keep their "hands" somewhere easily accessible, such as in their notebooks. From now on, any time a student needs a *Pat On The Back*, he can pull his "hand" out of his notebook and read the positive things that his peers have written about him.

The first point to ponder is that students can recognize the individuality and appreciate the strengths of their peers.

The second point to ponder is that what an individual gives is what she receives.

String Web

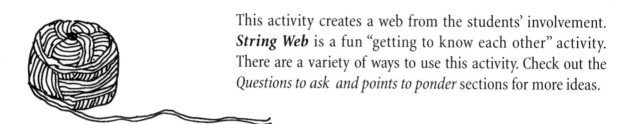

This activity creates a web from the students' involvement. *String Web* is a fun "getting to know each other" activity. There are a variety of ways to use this activity. Check out the *Questions to ask and points to ponder* sections for more ideas.

Materials needed

One ball of yarn is required for this activity.

Setting up the activity

The students and teacher will form a large circle in the center of the room, in the hallway, or outside. Students find it interesting and enjoyable to have their teacher involved.

Running the activity

The teacher should begin this activity by stating his or her name and something he or she likes that begins with the same letter of his or her name. For example, since Mrs. Booth likes baking, she would say, "Baking Mrs. Booth." Mrs. Booth then holds onto a piece of the yarn and tosses the ball of yarn to another player. The student must first state the name and "like" of Mrs. Booth and then state his or her own name and "like." The second person holds onto the yarn before tossing it to another player. The next player must try to recall the first two players and their "likes" before continuing the process. Each player must try to recall all players and their "likes." Example: "Baking Mrs. Booth, and I am Baseball Bob."

Processing the activity

When the activity is complete, a *String Web* is formed. Students quickly realize that the students at the beginning of the web had an easier task than those at the end. Follow up this activity with a discussion on mnemonic devices and memorization skills. Students also will begin to see a connection to other members in the class, and they will have fun during this process.

Questions to ask and points to ponder

This activity is helpful for learning names and encouraging team building. One variation is to call out the "like" and name of only the previous person rather than remembering facts for the entire class. Teachers have also varied this activity later in the year by having students pass the yarn ball to someone while making a positive comment about that student.

Example: Suzy starts, tosses the ball to Jane, and says, "I like how you always help other kids with math," or "I like how you always smile." This variation of the activity encourages a positive atmosphere in any classroom.

As a follow-up activity, the **String Web** may be taped to a large poster or banner and students may write their name in their place in the web. This follow-up activity creates an interesting visual that includes all members of a class or group.